CW00420336

I Wanted a Boat—So I Built One

This book is dedicated to Barbara, Betty, Rachel and Reuben

Copyright © 2022 Michael, Malcolm and Jonathan Emery

ISBN 978 1 909796 96 6

All rights reserved. No part of this publication may be reproduced, stored in a retrieval system or transmitted by any means, mechanical, photocopying, recording or otherwise, without the written permission of the publishers.

Designed and typeset in 11 on 12.65 Gilgamesh Pro by Poppyland Publishing.

The photographs used in this book are mostly from the Emery Family Archive. Those from other sources are listed as follows:

Archant Community Media Ltd 31, 59; Richard Batson 89, back cover; Brian Coe (film) 77 two right columns; David Cleveland 58; Bill Craske 35 bottom centre; Cromer Museum 21; Cyril Southerland 56 top and centre, 59; David Davies 78; Olive Edis 15, 75; Emery collection 4, 8, 13, 15 middle, 16, 18, 23, 26, 28, 29 right, 32-33, 35 top left and right, 37 top right, 38 centre right and bottom, 39, 41-55, 59 top left and right, 60, 61 above, centre and bottom left, 62, 63 above, 65-66, 68, 70 top left, 71, 72 right top and bottom, 73 top and centre right, 76, 77 left, 80-86, 87-88; David Hewitt 38 top right, 63 bottom left; Richard Loose 56 bottom left, 57; Diana McCallum 37, below and left; Norfolk Heritage Centre 25; Science Museum 36; Sheringham Museum 6, 11, 14; Peter Stibbons 29 left, 70 centre and bottom, 72 left, 73 bottom right; Poppyland Publishing 3, 61 bottom right; Neil Storey 64; Robin and Linda West 17, 70 top right; Philip Vicary 73 bottom left.

If you have any information, photos or memories of Sheringham built boats we would be pleased to hear from you. You can contact us on the following email address and we will endeavour to reply as quickly as possible:

emeryboats@outlook.com

www.iwantedaboat.co.uk

I Wanted a Boat—So I Built One

The story of the Emery family boatbuilding business

Michael, Malcolm and Jonathan Emery

POPPYLAND PUBLISHING

Built by Shannocks, crewed by Shannocks, the lifeboat *Henry Ramey Upcher*—when boats were wooden and crews were iron. A photo probably by Olive Edis.

From the era of the sailing crab boats with their single dipping lugsail, through the Sheringham private lifeboat *Henry Ramey Upcher* (launching behind the lugsail) to the time of engines and pot-haulers, the Emery family of Sheringham led the way. For a century this family's story is at the heart of Sheringham.

Contents

Preface

The Emery family's history of boat-building in Sheringham stretches back to around 1850. The idea for this book is a little newer—at 40 years old.

The death of Harold Emery in 1981 saw the closure of the workshop and the business after four generations and a century of craftsmanship.

Ever since then the current Emery clan—Michael, Malcolm and Jonathan—have been keen to capture their ancestors' legacy in print.

It aims to be something more permanent and explanatory than the piles of photos, cuttings, memories and anecdotes they cherish but have never put down in black and white for posterity.

Retired builder Michael, Harold's son, remembers the boats being built in the family boatshed—where he hunkered down under a hull after school to help hammer nails into another clinker built classic fishing boat. "I can still smell the wood in my nostrils," he says.

It was Malcolm, a former fisherman better known these days as entertainer and musician Razz the Clown, who said "We must get this down."

And it is Jonathan, Sheringham Little Theatre's former technical manager and projectionist, who has led their efforts to research, augment and order the family's story.

It is a story of men who crafted fishing boats by eye without plans—probably because they would not have been able to read them anyway—who used their skills, seafaring knowledge and ingenuity to build boats that were the workhorses of the Norfolk coast inshore fishing fleet.

Some of them still sail today, mainly for leisure. This book aims to keep the family's legacy afloat too.

It cannot be a fully-documented history—because chunks of it are missing as memories and records died with the people involved. But we have done our best to tell the tale of our family history—of which we are justifiably proud.

We hope you enjoy the voyage of reading it, savouring the pictures, embracing the memories of an era never to be repeated and smelling the wood in your nostrils.

Michael, Malcolm and Jonathan Emery 2022.

Opposite: Founder of the business Lewis 'Buffalo' Emery (centre) with his son Robert next to him, during the construction of the *Henry Ramey Upcher* private lifeboat in 1894. On the right is his eleven-year-old grandson Reginald and to Reginald's right is the vessel's first coxswain, Tom Barnes Cooper.

Meet the Family

The boat-building members of the Emery family

For a century the Emery family built boats that earned livelihoods and saved lives. The men who fashioned them were all craftsmen and some were colourful characters. Let us introduce them to you first in a family tree and then with snapshots of their lives.

Lewis 'Buffalo'

Robert 'Cally'

James Lewis 'Jimmy'

Reginald 'Young Cally'

Chris

Harold

Lifeboat or crab boat—see page 56—the launch and recovery of beach boats is the most difficult moment. Here a 'pushing off pole'—a quant—is used to provide initial momentum for the Emery-built lifeboat *Henry Ramey Upcher*.

A Century Of Craftmanship

They built their fishing boats without any drawn plans—just working with a finely-tuned craftsman's eye, and a knowledge of what their seafaring community needed in their workaday vessels.

But they were innovators too—hatching a design to help switch crab boats from sail to motor power, and exporting as far as the Falkland Islands.

The Emery family's boats across a century stretching from the 1850s to the 1950s were renowned for their quality—and some still exist today, giving pleasure to leisure sailors

The workshop where they were created, now a plush home with a stunning sea-view balcony, looked chaotic—but, at their height, it produced a dozen boats a year for fishermen of Norfolk and the east coast.

Their work also included one of the town's pioneering lifeboats, the *Henry Ramey Upcher*—which can be seen in the town's lifeboat museum trail.

The men who made them included top craftsmen and colourful characters, one with a penchant for a pint and a singalong, working until their seventies, even despite sight loss.

They were also involved in the tourism industry, renting out deck chairs and tents on the beach of Sheringham, as the town they worked and lived in morphed from a quiet fishing village to a busy holiday resort.

Their dynasty continues but the family nowadays works in other areas including music and entertainment.

They are proud of their ancestors' legacy to the boat-building and fishing world and the area's rich seafaring heritage—which is why they have decided to capture those halcyon days in this book.

The pictures and stories handed down through the Emery family help paint a picture of their vital contribution to the industry, and give a snapshot of the times they lived and worked in.

Lewis 'Buffalo' Emery (1817–1902)

"I wanted a boat so I built one"

by Michael Emery

The Emery family's voyage into boat-building began around 1850—through a combination of necessity, determination and enterprising 'diversification' of carpentry skills into a new arena … on the high seas.

Lewis Emery was the son of Benjamin, a Norwich 'carrier' cart driver, and Sarah Grimes, who lived at East Beckham. He became a carpenter and fisherman who around 1850 wanted a new boat but could not get anyone to build him one.

So he decided to build himself a boat. And it was a good one. Other fishermen were soon asking if he would build them a boat too, which saw him switch from fishing and go into boat-building full-time.

Lewis had a large family of four sons and three daughters. The four sons James, Robert, Ben and John ('Mad Jack') went on to help him, with Robert later taking over. They worked from a shed near the West End gangway.

Their growing reputation meant that when Sheringham needed to replace its first private lifeboat the *Augusta*, which was suffering from 'nail sickness' and generally falling apart, Lewis was approached by the donor, Lady Caroline Upcher of Sheringham Hall, and offered the job of building a new one.

Lewis was 77 when, on April 4th, 1894, he began laying the keel from a perfect piece of oak, which he had acquired in Great Yarmouth. He was helped by his son Robert who was credited with the actual design of the vessel, and his other sons along with brother George at times and Harry Diver from Great Yarmouth. The new lifeboat was launched and named by the donor on September 4th, 1894. It was named *Henry Ramey Upcher* after Lady Caroline Upcher's late husband. The vessel went on to save 202 lives during 56 years of service and can still be viewed, preserved in its original shed at the top of the West End fishermen's slope.

Lewis was also involved in building work in the town and was heavily involved in the construction of the original Upcher groyne, one of the first sea defence breakwaters to be built on the Sheringham beach. Sadly this was demolished to make way for a replacement when there appeared to be nothing wrong with the original. A piece of Sheringham history gone!

The Emerys also became linked with another famous fishing family from the town. Lewis's daughter Florence, by his second wife Ann (his first wife Sarah had died childless), married Henry 'Downtide' West senior. They had a son Henry, also later nicknamed 'Downtide', who became a fish merchant, fisherman and coxswain of the Sheringham RNLI boat *Foresters' Centenary*.

Lewis's daughter Elizabeth married Benjamin Joseph Harrison of Cromer which would have been a rare occurrence in those days of intense rivalry between the two towns.

What's in a Name?

So how did 'Buffalo' Emery get his name? The north Norfolk coast is not renowned for having herds of powerful horned beasts more familiar on the plains of Africa and America.

A family anecdote says it stems back from when Lewis Emery is said to have carried a huge heavy ship's vice up the beach at Sheringham on his back. The tool, set on wheels, was hauled around the deck of a ship to carry out repair and maintenance jobs.

Lewis salvaged one from a shipwreck on the beach and added it to his workshop (it is now in the town museum along with other tools) and the act of getting it from shore to shed led to someone saying to Lewis, "you're as strong as a buffalo."

No-one knows if it is true, but it's the best explanation the family has—and a great story.

During lean times the family took on other building work. Lewis was the carpenter involved in building Sheringham's first United Methodist Free Chapel which was opened on December 22nd, 1858. It was located in what is now New Road behind the *Robin Hood* public house.

During the 1920s the family were also involved with the Arts and Crafts architect John Sydney Brocklesby. John, who lived in the London borough of Merton, built houses in St Austin's Grove, Sheringham, and various other places around the neighbourhood.

He also purchased most of the properties in Gun Street and Lifeboat Plain including the workshops and Govan Cottage where the Emery family lived and worked. The property was mortgaged to Reginald 'young Cally' and paid back over the years, finally being wound up on his death in 1957. Reginald was John Brocklesby's agent in Sheringham, collecting rents from the holiday lets and rented accommodation in the locality. They also carried out repairs to some of the properties, which would interrupt work on whichever boats were being built at the time, much to the annoyance of the customers no doubt. Another building they carried out work on was Abbey House in Abbey Road.

Reginald's eldest son John Robert (known as Bob), and his wife Hilda, also worked for Brocklesby—especially after he purchased the nearby redundant Weybourne Mill, which he restored in the mid 1920s and used as his north Norfolk base. Bob was involved with the restoration of the mill, and also worked on other building projects in Norfolk. Hilda was cook for the Brocklesby family that lived there during the summer months.

Robert 'Cally' William West Emery (1863—1941)

Remembered by Chris and Michael Emery

He was renowned as the best boat-builder in the family—but also as a character with a liking for drink and singing.

Robert was known as 'Cally'—because of the Norfolk dialect description of his short tight curly ('Cally') hair. One claim to fame came in 1914 when the Sheringham fish merchant H. R. Johnson wanted to find a way of installing Belfast-Barker two-stroke motors into the sailing crab boats to help them travel faster and work further from shore. Robert was tasked with finding a way for the propeller shaft to be put through the stern of the boat, while protecting its blades from being damaged by the stones when being hauled up the beach.

He is said to have lain in bed one night and dreamed up the design for a "beautiful starnpost" as reported in his obituary. The design went on to be used for different vessel types around the country. Lack of money prevented Robert from taking out a patent on his design which could have earned him more money but he was still pleased with his invention.

Robert, whose family nickname was 'D D', was also a keen model-maker and one of his models of a Sheringham sailing crab boat resides in the Science Museum in London. To travel he always went for the train a half hour or so early, maintaining that it might come early!

'Cally' liked his beer and was said to work better drunk. He spent a lot of his time, and his money, in the *Crown* public house where Charley Holsey was landlord. Patrons enjoyed encouraging him to sing the song *Baltimore* from the top of a bar table—which he did with all his might. His favourite song however was *Kelly from the Isle of Man*.

On a Saturday he would take grandson Chris to Overstrand to carry out repairs to the boats there. Chris would end up sitting outside the local public house whilst 'Cally' would "just go in here for a little while". He normally emerged at closing time so no repairs would be carried out that day. "Never mind bor, we'll come back next Saturday", he would say.

Tom Dennis of Overstrand remembered being asked by his father to go meet Mr Emery from Overstrand railway station and carry his tool box. On arrival he found Robert holding just a small carpenter's bag containing a saw, hammer, length of wood and a few copper nails amongst the sawdust. He travelled light.

He wore a trilby most of the time, but on Saturday's he would don his best bowler and go to Cromer by train to ask a customer for some money to carry on with construction of his new crab boat. One Sheringham fisherman remembered him asking another fisherman, "Can you give me three pounds to purchase the oak for the keel". On receiving the money he would make his way to the *Crown* and spend the money on a drink or two! Robert would later go back to the fisherman and ask for more money to buy timber for the planking and ribs, and so it went on. In those days, when a boat cost a pound a foot, the original quote, if there was one, would never be met.

Robert, always keen to use materials around him for 'admin', would sometimes write the quote on the back of a door at the workshop. Once, when in need of something to jot some plans on, he reportedly used a board that had recently been used to carry away casualties from a fatal explosion at the nearby seafront sewage disposal tank on May 1st, 1903, which killed three people and severely injured several more.

He would start work when it suited him, often after a session in the pub, which meant that you could probably find him in the workshop working late at night by candle light. Passers-by recalled hearing him singing his head off as he worked.

Robert told the story of how he once extended the length of a boat for 'Go-Father' Pegg by splicing four foot in the middle all in secret. No one ever saw it done!! But he told the story.

Another favourite habit was chewing tobacco, quite often chewing then spitting it onto the wall. When it was dry he would press it in his clay pipe and smoke it. One fisherman could remember finding quite a lot of tobacco in the bottom of his new vessel.

The upper floor of his boat-building shed on Lifeboat Plain had previously been the meeting house of the Salvation Army. When its band came down to Lifeboat Plain to play for an anniversary event, Robert is reported to have called out to them: "There have been more swear words in here than there have been prayer words since you left". It did not go down too well!

Whilst working on a boat that was ordered for the Falkland Islands, the copper nails would sometimes bend and refuse to go into the planks, and Robert would exclaim: "There you are bor, another nail that doesn't want to go away to the Falklands."

An incident involving repairs to the *Henry Ramey Upcher* had a less than happy ending. Robert was laying by the keel and son Reginald was inside hammering copper nails through. Unfortunately Robert was too close to the keel and a nail came through and pierced the corner of his eye which lost its sight. He had a spell in Norwich hospital but suffered severe pain from the accident for a long time after.

Thankfully, now being blind in one eye didn't affect his judgement and the boats he turned out were as good as they had always been.

It didn't affect his sense of humour either. He reportedly once told his two grandsons after the accident: "I can see more with my one eye than you can with your two because you can only see one of my eyes and I can see two of yours".

His dry wit and wisdom also saw him tell them: "I've taught you everything I know, and you still don't know nothing."

Sadly, towards the end of his life the sight in his remaining eye failed, but he carried on working by touch until his death, when son Reginald took over the business.

In 1905 the famous composer Ralph Vaughan Williams visited the *Crown* pub while travelling the country recording traditional folk tunes for posterity before they disappeared. Robert sang another one of his songs, *Near Scarborough Town*, to Vaughan Williams so that he could note down the tune. The composer later spent some time in Sheringham working on one of his symphonies between 1919 and 1921.

James 'Jimmy' Lewis Emery (1861—1948)

Jimmy joined the business early on with his father, Lewis and brother, Robert. Then in 1891, possibly during a lean time in the fishing industry and a fall in demand for new boats, he left and borrowed £20 to set up as a builder. This was during the time that north Norfolk was experiencing a boom in construction as the area became popular through the 'Poppyland' writings of Clement Scott, which attracted new waves of holidaymakers and incoming residents. Unfortunately by 1894 Jimmy had got into serious financial difficulties. By his own admission he knew nothing about estimating for building houses, and very little about bricks and mortar, when he started out. All his contracts made a loss and with mounting debts, not to mention a £60 doctor's bill due to his wife Eliza suffering from a period of illness, he was declared bankrupt in 1895.

He worked when required in the family business including helping in the construction of the *Henry Ramey Upcher* lifeboat. His main income was from his skills making furniture and model boats.

Eighty–three year old Jimmy in 1943 with a model crab boat which he bequeathed to Beeston Road Methodist church. Standing behind him is his great nephew Sidney, home on leave from service in the Royal Navy.

Reginald 'Young Cally' Edward Emery (1883–1957)

Reg, photographed by Olive Edis

Memories by Michael Emery told to him by his father Harold.

Reg, the son of Robert and Maria, went to school at Upper Sheringham before joining the family boat-building firm in 1894. He worked with grandfather, Lewis 'Buffalo' Emery on the rowing and sailing lifeboat *Henry Ramey Upcher*, and many more builds thereafter.

When Lewis retired in 1896 Reg worked with his father Robert who became proprietor of the business which by now had moved to Lifeboat Plain. Also working in the firm was Reginald's uncle, James.

Fishing was one of the main industries in Sheringham at the turn of the century, so they were kept busy on the building of crab and whelk boats. In 1910 Reg married Priscilla Starling from Norwich and they started married life living in a cottage at the bottom of Gun Street, Sheringham.

At the outbreak of the First World War Reg was sent to Scotland to work in the shipyards of Messrs. Fairfield at Govan, a name he gave to his cottage on his return (Govan Cottage). He was involved in the construction of ships' lifeboats.

Reg had a large family of eight children two of which—Harold and Chris—would join him in the business in the late 1920s. Things were in full swing by now, building up to twelve boats a year, mostly crabbers, with the occasional whelker. From early in that decade Reg rented out beach tents and deck chairs in the summer months assisted by his wife, Priscilla. He also made wooden framed canvas beach tents.

Reg and wife Priscilla, Sheringham east promenade

In his spare time Reg—with his father Robert and later with his son Reginald junior—was a member of the Sheringham Rocket Brigade, which fired rescue lines from the shore to stricken ships close to shore. He was also a keen bowls player in his younger days.

After the death of his father Robert in 1941 Reg became the head of the firm, working with his two sons Harold and Chris, after they came back from war work at Oulton Broad. The first boat constructed after the war was a motor crab boat for Reg's son Sidney. After Chris left the firm in 1954, Reg and Harold carried on the business.

In January of 1957 Reg's wife Priscilla died and this was too much for him. He never went near the workshops again, and Harold had to finish the final boat *Charles Mark* off himself.

Reg had one other sibling, a brother also named Robert who was unable to join the family business as there was not enough work for them all. But he was able to continue the Emery boat-building tradition elsewhere. When he left school his mother Maria bought him an apprenticeship with a firm at Wroxham working on the construction of the famous Broads Brown Boats. Later in his career he moved to Oulton Broad to work for Brooke Marine, constructing boats there and thus establishing the Lowestoft branch of the family.

Harold Spencer Emery (1912–1981)

by Michael Emery

Harold officially joined the business in 1928 after leaving school aged 14, but he had already been 'hanging around' the workshop and learning for years.

He was born in April 1912 in Govan Cottage, Gun Street, Sheringham to Reginald and Priscilla Emery. Harold attended Sheringham School in Barford Road, where he was a keen footballer and played in the school team.

He worked alongside grandfather Robert, the proprietor, his father Reginald and great uncle James. His brother Chris would join the business about three years later. They worked at the building of crab and whelk boats for the fishermen along the north Norfolk Coast.

When not at work he continued his interest in football and played for teams in the area. In 1938 he married Doris Blogg from Cromer, whose father was cousin to the great lifeboatman Henry Blogg.

They started married life living at 22, Cliff Road, Sheringham. At the outbreak of the Second World War Harold was called up for war work with his brother Chris and sent to work at Brooke Marine at Oulton Broad on the building of Motor Torpedo Boats (MTBs). For a short time he also worked in a munitions factory in Stoke, before returning to Brooke Marine until the end of the war. During the war Harold had two sons, Michael in 1940 and Richard in 1942, both born at Cliff Road.

At the end of the war it was back to Sheringham and the family business which was by now being run by his father Reginald. The business resumed with Reginald, Harold and Chris in 1946. The first boat built was the *Enterprise* for Harold's brother Sid who was being discharged from the Royal Navy.

Harold had by now moved from Cliff Road to 25, The Avenue where another son Trevor was born. He also took up golf, joining the Sheringham Artisans and later Sheringham Golf Club, playing the game to a handicap of 11. His sons Richard and Trevor followed him into the sport—and did even better. Richard went on to become a professional golfer, and Trevor played for Norfolk many times.

The boat-building was not as busy as before the Second World War, with production down from 12 to two a year. To supplement income Harold would rent out beach huts and hire out deck chairs during the summer months. In the early 50s he also invested in floats for hire.

Harold's brother Chris left the firm in the early 1950s. With Harold and father Reg still at the helm, the boat-building was down to just one boat a year, meaning Harold was more reliant on the beach hut business. In 1957 Reg died, leaving Harold as the sole proprietor. He continued doing boat repairs—signalling the end of more than 100 years of Emery boat-building tradition.

When Harold died aged 67 in 1981 the family business came to a full stop—its work well done and not forgotten.

Harold appears to be performing acrobatics from a ladder whilst the whelker *William Edward* is being fitted out on the *Windham Arms* car park next to the workshops in 1949.

Christopher Alfred Emery (1913—1987)

Chris joined the business soon after leaving school to work alongside his brother, father and grandfather. In 1940 Chris married Elizabeth Ayres from Burnham Market, but sadly they were never blessed with any children.

During the Second World War Chris and his brother Harold carried out their war service at Brooke Marine in Lowestoft where they worked on building Motor Torpedo Boats (MTBs). Coincidentally, while Chris and Harold were working on MTBs their brother Sidney was serving in the Royal Navy on one of the vessels that they had helped build.

Following war service Chris returned to Sheringham and the family business, continuing until the early 1950s when the fishing industry and its need for new boats was declining. The business was not making enough to keep three families, so Chris left to work on the local airbases as a carpenter. He ended his career working in the maintenance department of Her Majesty's Stationery Office in Norwich.

Retirement saw Chris carrying on the family business of letting deck chairs and beach huts on the East End promenade. He stored these in his shed at the top of the West Cliff fishermen's slope. Here he also could be found carrying out various repairs on the boats of local fishermen when needed. With the death of Chris in 1987, Sheringham lost its last link with boat-building in the town.

Second left: Chris outside his shed at the top of the West End gangway with a rudder he had made for fisherman Peter Scotter's boat, *Windsor Rose*. Left: A 'wrong' made by Chris for fisherman Richard Little's boat. A 'wrong' is placed inside towards the stem of a boat to give extra support when beaching on the shingle beaches at Sheringham.

Lewis the Exhibitionist Inventor

Research for this book has thrown up some new facts previously unknown to the current family. The model-making skills of Robert Emery are mentioned elsewhere—but Lewis 'Buffalo' Emery's skills at making miniature, as well as full-scale boats, has also been discovered. Newspaper reports revealed Lewis had been an inventor and model-maker—passing on those skills to at least two of his sons. He exhibited a full-size crab boat and model of an improved self-righting lifeboat at three prestigious national and international exhibitions as well as in his home county. The Norwich and Eastern Counties Industrial Exhibition was held at St. Andrew's Hall in Norwich from Wednesday August 14th to Thursday September 26th, 1867. The *Norfolk Chronicle* dated Saturday, August 24th, 1867 noted:

> L. Emery, boat-builder, Sherringham [sic], exhibits a clever model of an improved life-boat for the Eastern Coast, on the self-righting principle, securing a large breadth of beam, his own invention.

The edition of Saturday, September 7th added that Lewis had received "The Very Rev. the Dean of Norwich's prize of £3 3s., and medal for the model which was entry number 572."

In 1881 St. Andrew's Hall in Norwich was the venue for the National Fisheries Exhibition held from Easter Monday, April 18th to Saturday, May 7th, and Lewis exhibited there too. The *Norfolk News* edition of Saturday, April 23rd, 1881 recorded:

> Mr L. Emery, Sherringham, a clench-built boat, 17 ft. in length, with necessary fittings.

The *Field Gentleman's Newspaper* of Saturday, April 30th, 1881 gave more detail of the boat:

> Lewis Emery, Lower Sherringham, Cromer, sends a clench-built boat of oak, wherry sterned, 17 ft. in length by 7 ft. 2in. in beam, with fittings, bottom boards, and gear. This boat has great rise of floor, although for use on a beach, and the reason is that the beach being steep, the boats rest against it with the shoulder when run ashore, and can be kept from listing off towards the surf, which would thus fill them at once, and might cause damage or loss in a heavy swell breaking on the shore.

The *Lowestoft Journal* of April 23rd added that in the models section:

> Mr. L. Emery — the old Sherringham life boat, designed [sic] in 1838 by Mr. Upcher, and found to be most effective.

And the *Norfolk News* of the same day said,

> A model of the *Augusta* Life-boat, built by the Hon. Mrs. Sherringham [sic] in 1838, a boat which has been instrumental in saving many lives, stands alongside the Institution [RNLI] model.

Because of the inaccuracies in both of these articles it will be interesting to discover if Lewis had made and exhibited a model of Sheringham's first private lifeboat.

Due to the success of the Norwich Exhibition of 1881, in 1883 the Great International Fisheries Exhibition was held in South Kensington, London. It ran from Saturday, May 12th until Wednesday, October 31st, 1883. The official catalogue lists Lewis as having two exhibits:

186. EMERY, LEWIS, Sherringham, Norwich. Norfolk Crab Boat, fitted with fishing gear. (Lewis was awarded a bronze medal for this.)

363. EMERY, LEWIS, Sherringham, Norwich. Model of a Life-boat, fitted with tank to ballast with water when afloat.

An interesting account in the *Sporting Life* on Thursday, May 24th, 1883 says:

> Lewis Emery, of Sherringham, Norwich, and a silver medallist at the Exhibition held there, shows a Norfolk crab boat with rowlock holes in the sides, in lieu of the usual thole pins. The inventor of this idea claims for it that it is much safer for rowing purposes, and particularly when the sea is rough, than the ordinary style.

So it would seem Lewis was the first to introduce rowlock holes into the Norfolk crab boats, an idea taken from the Viking long ships of centuries before.

The *Eastern Evening News* edition of Monday, June 24th, 1883 refers to:

> The various cunning contrivances for catching crustaceans.

> Numerous new varieties are being introduced among English fishermen, or are at any rate on view at the Exhibition, in competition for the prize for lobster and crab-pots which will permit the escape of under-sized crustaceans. Messrs. Lewis Emery & Son of Sherringham exhibits the character of boat and gear used by the crab and lobster catchers at that important fishing village. The crab and lobster pot has the flat bottom, the arched roof, with the opposite funnel-shaped entrances. However, despite the Emery efforts, the prize was awarded to Mr. De Caux of Yarmouth.

> Whelk traps are shown, one by Mr. Emery, to illustrate the mode of catching what many fishermen regard only as bait, but what in London is a very popular dish, partaken of al fresco.

Appearing at such exhibitions was an important chance to showcase new ideas and products—a bit like the modern-day International Boat Show—particularly for a family of humble fisherfolk and craftsmen from North Norfolk.

And major efforts were made to help impoverished fishermen to attend them, as a report from the *Eastern Daily Press* on Saturday, May 5th, 1883 shows. Under the heading Local Topics, writer C. L. T notes:

> I observe that Mr. I. O. Howard Taylor is appealing for support to the fund for sending the Norfolk fishermen to the International Exhibition in London. Sixteen specimens of this hardy tribe of sea-wrestlers are to be sent from the Norfolk coast to the metropolis. The Great Eastern Railway Company will convey them gratis. They are to be boarded, lodged, and shown the big things of the great city in connection with their calling, and thus have a pleasant trip and a profitable time. Their ordinary life is full of hardship and peril. The generous residents of the county and city will respond to Mr. Taylor's appeal to assist in giving them a few fair days to light their stormy years.

Some 400 fishermen attended the opening from Britain and Ireland.

It is hoped the Norfolk contingent of *"sea wrestlers"* had a good and educational visit before returning to their life of hardship and peril.

From the left: Joe Sayer (Cromer Haulier), Robert Emery, John 'Snouts' Cox, John 'Tar' Bishop (Sheringham fisherman and sail maker), Billy 'Shepherd' Hannah (Eastern Sea Fisheries Officer), Reginald Emery.

An unidentified Emery boat loaded onto a horse-drawn cart around the early 1900s. This was built for Cromer fisherman John 'Snouts' Cox. It is said that John had no fewer than 23 boats built, because other fishermen would rib him that there was something wrong with the finished boat. They would say that the keel wasn't straight or it was too beamy or too heavy for carrying up the beach. He would promptly sell the vessel and order a new one!

Contract to Build a Special Lifeboat

The flagship of the Emery-built fleet was undoubtedly the *Henry Ramey Upcher* lifeboat.

Because she was a lifeboat—saving scores of stricken seafarers in daring missions over four decades of service—she was bound to attract more attention than the journeyman fishing boats bringing crabs and whelks ashore that the Emery family was more used to building.

But the local squire's family from Sheringham Hall, who paid for the town's first two private lifeboats, chose Lewis 'Buffalo' Emery to build the new vessel because of his glowing reputation among the east coast fishing fraternity.

In November 1893 a deputation of fishermen met Henry Ramey Upcher's widow Caroline who agreed to pay for a replacement for the aging lifeboat *Augusta,* which the Upcher family also provided because of mounting concerns about fishermen's safety following a grim 1836 when seven men were lost in severe gales.

The *Henry Ramey Upcher* was again like a crab boat but twice the size, and—at 34 ft. 9in long and 11 ft. 3in wide in the beam—slightly larger than the *Augusta.* She also had copper fastenings rather than the rust-prone iron nails that saw the *Augusta* fail. For increased stability, the *Ramey* had built-in copper tanks for buoyancy chambers and a cork belt covered in canvas around the outside.

Lewis was a sprightly 77 when given the task—but was helped by his brother George and sons Robert, James, John and Ben. A 46-year-old shipwright, Harry Diver from Great Yarmouth, was involved with the construction. It is believed he was probably known to Lewis's nephew George, a saddler by trade who had moved his family to Great Yarmouth to make a living there.

It took months to find a suitable piece of wood for the keel —a length of imported American oak from Great Yarmouth. But after the ceremonial driving of the first nail by members of the Upcher family on April 4th, 1894 she was launched, at 12 minutes past midday, exactly five months later on September 4th, 1894. Large crowds lining the cliffs and gangway also saw her give a demonstration with a crew of 30 using sail and oar.

The 'HRU' carried out 56 services, saving 202 lives, many of them local fishermen. She worked alongside the new RNLI boats for many years, but was often faster to launch as she was lighter.

Although she was a very steady and safe boat, and particularly good under sail, the *Henry Ramey Upcher* was considered a hard boat to row.

Her most notable rescue was on January 23rd, 1897, when she helped the Norwegian brig *Ispolen* which was blown ashore in a gale. The RNLI slipway had been washed away so their boat was having to be man-handled through the town to another gangway. In the meantime the *HRU* launched with coxswain Barnes Cooper at the helm.

Two oars were broken and a fender damaged as the *HRU* smashed into the brig on the first attempt to come alongside in high seas. The second attempt got grappling hooks on to the casualty and the lifeboat hauled alongside—despite danger from damaged masts. The Norwegian crew of eight jumped to safety and were taken to the *Two Lifeboats* coffee room for hot food and dry clothes. The ship was smashed to pieces but a few ribs from her hulk remain visible today at low tides.

The *Henry Ramey Upcher* retired from active service in 1935, giving way to the RNLI. Ten years later she was launched to celebrate VJ day—Victory over Japan—to mark the end of the Second World War. But it was an ignominious final journey. Overladen with 56 passengers in worsening weather she bowed out, having to be helped home by the RNLI crew

The *HRU* was stored, and almost forgotten in her shed, until it was restored as a museum in the mid-1970s. It was later taken over by the Preservation Society and remains a popular attraction today preserving an important chapter of Sheringham's lifeboat heritage and the star of the Emery boat-building story.

Jimmy 'Coaley' Cooper and Reginald Emery pose with the *Henry Ramey Upcher* lifeboat. Jimmy was the vessel's last coxswain (1900–1935).

The Introduction of Motors

The biggest single development in the unchanging double-ended fishing boat that served generations was down to fisherman Harry Johnson—and the skills of the Emery family. Known as 'Knicker-bockers' due to his preferred choice of trouser, even on the beach, H. R. Johnson is credited with introducing motor power to a craft traditionally driven by sail and oar. But it could not have happened without the craftsmanship of Robert Emery who found a way to incorporate "modern technology" into a time-honoured design.

Here is how the story unfolded.

Harry Johnson, the main fish merchant of Sheringham, wanted to increase the catches of the local sailing boats by fitting engines. This would allow the boats to go out in less favourable weather and farther afield to new lucrative fishing grounds as well as carry a larger catch to meet the growing local and national market for shellfish and fish from north Norfolk.

Harry's first attempt was in 1905 when he had a 35 ft. boat built by William Spence of Southtown, Great Yarmouth. This was referred to as a Sheringham Yawl, built to the design of the beach yawls used on that part of the coast, and named *Reaper*.

It was fitted with a 15 h.p. Gardner motor which was capable of giving a speed of between seven and eight miles an hour. There was also a small auxiliary 2 h.p. paraffin motor for driving a winch or pot-hauler. Interestingly, though the fitting of a pot-hauler was quite an innovation for the time, it would be over thirty years before pot-haulers were re-introduced to the local boats. Fitted with a Gaines reversible propeller, *Reaper* also carried two lug-sails in case there were problems with the motor.

To be used for shrimping and whelking, *Reaper* was launched on Tuesday March 7th, 1905. Why he chose the style of boat and where his advice came from is not clear. The vessel was too large for beach use so was worked from Blakeney Harbour. Over time it became apparent that *Reaper* had no real advantages over the local sailing boats to justify its continued use. Harry must have written it off as a failure and its eventual fate is unknown.

News of the boat featured in a short article in the *Illustrated London News* of March 1905, and the *Eastern Daily Press* also in March of that year.

The idea remained festering in his mind over the next few years until Harry wrote a letter to the magazine the *Motor Ship and Motor Boat*, about the experimental technology of using an aeroplane-style propeller to power a marine vessel. This appeared in the October, 1913 edition.

Aerial Propulsion

Sir,—I am interested in small fishing boats fishing from the shore which have to be beached every day, very often in rough weather on a rough, pebbly beach. These boats have to go a distance up to 12 miles under sail and oars, and if possible, I should like to introduce motors for them. They are about 20 ft. long with 6 ft. 6 in. beam, and of the double-ended type. The difficulty is that there is no harbour, and the usual kind of installation with propeller under water is no good, as when the boats were beached damage would be caused. I am wondering whether a detachable motor would be of any use, but am afraid that in the hands of unskilled men like fishermen this would not be a success, as the motor would have to be laid in the open boat amongst the pots, lines, etc. I am also informed that aerial propulsion has been tried

Reaper on the day of her launch, Tuesday March 7th 1905 on the river Yare, Great Yarmouth.

and found successful. If you could give me any information as to this or refer me to a firm experimenting I should be glad. It seems to me that this arrangement, if possible, would be just the thing for my purpose.—Yours faithfully, H.R. Johnson.

[We should think a detachable motor might prove satisfactory, but should not advise you to fit one of less than 3 h.p. For rough usage it is better to have a permanently installed motor, and the beaching trouble could be got over by building a boat with a large amount of outside dead wood completely surrounding the propeller and so protecting it from damage. Regarding aerial propellers, Mr. T. W. K. Clark, of 29, High Street, Hampton Wick, has had experience in work of this nature, and might be able to give you an estimate for suitable plants. If you decide to make inquiries regarding this we would advise you to employ motors of 6 h.p. , which would probably give the boat a speed of 4 ½ or 5 knots, or, say, 5 to 6 m.p.h.—Ed]

We are not certain whether Aerial Propulsion—as used in American Everglades 'air boats'—was ever tried on the local boats, but it is probable that the costs of such experimental equipment would have been prohibitive

There followed two further articles in the same magazine. The first was in August, 1914.

Motor Installation in a Beach Boat.

At the beginning of the present season, Mr H. Johnson of Sheringham, Norfolk, wrote as to the possibility of installing some of the beaching cobles with a motor, the main obstacles in the way of success being the question of protecting the propeller, when launching and hauling up, and also the difficulty of keeping the engine free from salt water, as there is generally a considerable "run" on the beach.

After going into the matter Mr. Johnson decided that one of Messrs. Norris, Henty and Gardner's Belfast-Barker two-stroke motors, of about 6 h.p. size, would be most suitable. An order for one of these sets was placed, and this was installed in one of the existing cobles, the *Columbia*, owned by Mr. E. Cooper, and from the day of trials she proved herself to be a success in every way, as she was able to get out and fish her pots when other boats could not do so on account of adverse winds.

There are now five or six new boats building and on order to be installed with motors, and last week a similar boat, slightly larger, was launched with a 10 h.p. engine. Messrs. Long, Craske and Love have a new boat nearly finished at Mr. C.

One half of *Coaley* is seen here in a Sheringham garden on November 13th, 1983. A number of vessels ended their days in this way, used as summer houses.

Emerson's [sic] yard, to be fitted with a 6 h.p. Belfast-Barker outfit, and Mr. J. Cooper is also installing a 4 h.p. outfit of the same make in his coble "*Coaley.*"

The fishing ground is seven or eight miles from shore, and as there is practically no shelter of any kind the boats must necessarily be good sea boats and equipped with a very reliable engine. They carry on an average 1½ tons of whelks.

The boat referred to as being built for Long, Craske and Love was *Welcome Home.* As noted in Robert Emery's profile earlier, he is said to have lain in bed thinking up the design for his thicker stern post in order that a propeller could be safely protected from the pebble beaches at Sheringham, as used in *Welcome Home.*

The second article appeared in the March, 1916 edition.

Motor Cobles on Norfolk Coast.

Since the introduction of motors in the beaching cobles of Sheringham, and the exceedingly good results obtained, great interest has been manifested by the fishermen at other parts of the coast, with the result that several of them have already had or are having engines installed.

At Brancaster Staithe there are four boats fitted with B.B. engines, one with a Kermath, one Daimler and one Gnome, making a fleet of seven boats equipped with motors in a few months. There are also three boats on order for the same port, all to be fitted with B.B. motors, also a larger type of decked boat owned by Mr. Will Loose is to be fitted with one of the slow-speed heavy-duty Gardner engines for trawling and oyster dredging.

There are building at Emery's yard two beaching cobles; one for Sheringham, and one for Cromer, both of which are to be fitted with B.B. motors of 4 h.p. and 6 h.p. respectively, and at J. Johnson's yard one boat for Brancaster and one for Sheringham to be similarly equipped.

It is wonderful what good sea boats these quite open type of craft are, going out in all kinds of weather, and it is interesting to note that recently one of these local motor boats took in tow the lifeboat, which is equipped only with oars and sails.

When it is remembered that a little over two years ago there were no motors installed in the cobles at Sheringham, we think all credit is due to Mr. H.R. Johnson, the local fish buyer, who gave the men a lead by equipping one of the boats at his own expense.

At Seaton, Devon, by the time these lines appear in print trials will have been run of a fine type of open beaching launch for fishing purposes for Mr. Head, of this town. The boat was built by Messrs. Levis and son, of Exmouth, and the B.B. motor supplied by Messrs. Trevett and Co., motor engineers, Seaton.

The article rightly gives credit to Harry Johnson for finally achieving his goal in fitting motors to the working boats of north Norfolk, and that Robert Emery's stern post design became universally adopted around the coasts of Britain for similar types of vessel.

Harry Johnson not only purchased and installed the motors for those fishermen that could not afford the outlay, his men also serviced them and he supplied the petrol. The fishermen were able to pay him back over time.

Left: *Welcome Home* outside the Lifeboat Plain workshops on launch day, Saturday September 5th, 1914. Robert Emery is to the right of the sternpost.

Right: The boat reaches the bottom of Coastguard Slip ready to be turned onto the shingle beach and launched into the North Sea for her maiden trip.

With many helpers the boat has reached the West Promenade just outside Flagstaff House. Robert Emery is at the stem of the boat wearing his bowler hat.

THE BOAT BIOGRAPHIES

QJ & J YH232 (Queenie, Jack and Jimmy)

A hoveller, built 1915 for John James Davies, Cromer.

John James worked the boat, which was one of the first to be fitted with a motor, from Cromer until 1931 when his step son, the famous Cromer lifeboatman, Henry Blogg, took over the ownership and used her until 1937. A hoveller was usually an unlicensed boat which was also used for cargo salvage work and to attend vessels in distress, helping the crews ashore safely. They had a forward cuddy like the later whelkers, so they could be used on longer journeys with the crew able to sleep or take shelter.

QJ & J was sold on to a Wells fisherman and used there for whelking until finally ending up as a pleasure craft in the Blackwater Estuary in Essex under the custodianship of Chris Smith and friends. Then, knowing of its Henry Blogg connection, members of the Sheringham Museum discovered that she was going to be broken up so set about bringing her back to the town for preservation. After several attempts, and now in a very precarious state, she was taken to the Museum of the Broads. Here it was decided that, due to her poor state, they would only be able save the front section of the hull. In 2016 the remaining 10 ft. restored bow section of the vessel was finally displayed next to the bust of Henry Blogg at North Lodge Park in Cromer.

The final journey. The restored front section of *QJ & J* is moved next to the bust of Henry Blogg at North Lodge Park, Cromer.

A Boat Built for the Falkland Islands

In 1928 Robert Emery had his first 'export order'—a boat for the Falkland Islands Company. How did a boat builder in north Norfolk land the task of providing a fishing vessel for use 8,000 miles away? The following report appeared in the *Norfolk Chronicle* on Friday September 14th of that year.

From Norfolk to the Falklands

Sheringham Built Boat Exported

Unique Event

An event probably unique in the history of North Norfolk occurred on Friday of last week when a motor fishing boat, built by Mr R. Emery of Gun Street, Sheringham, left Beach Station, Cromer at 2.50 pm on its way to Port Stephens, the Falkland Islands, ten thousand miles away.

The boat, which is of similar design to the most recently built local fishing boat, had been ordered for the Falkland Islands Co. Ltd., by a gentleman who had visited Cromer during winters for the past ten years, as being the best type of boat for the conditions obtaining in that little island within the British Empire.

The boat was tested by Coxswain Henry Blogg, the famous lifeboat hero, at Cromer, and was then hauled up the gangway by three horses, and put onto a flat machine truck at Beach Station, and sent to Liverpool, from whence it will be conveyed by the SS. *Orita*. With the boat is a two-wheeled carriage, similar in construction to that used for the Cromer lifeboat, *Louisa Heartwell*, with the exception that the latter has four wheels. This was hand-made by Mr. W.E. Rogers, coachbuilder, of Cromer. The two wheels are 5 ft. 6 ins. high, and the carriage will be used, it is understood to take the boat over rocky ground to the beach at the Falklands. The carriage left Beach Station on Saturday.

The approximate measurements of the boat which is oak built are: 18 ft. 7 ins. over all, 3 ft. 3¾ ins. deep, 6 ft. 10½ ins. wide and 12 ft. 3 ins. on the keel from stem to stern-post. This is the first time that a boat has been sent abroad from Sheringham although Mr. Emery has sent boats to various fishing places on the Yorkshire coast. The motor engine was made by Messrs. Brookes of Lowestoft.

In the same paper *A Norfolker's Diary* added:

That a Sheringham built boat should be sent to a port over seven thousand miles away is an event of considerable interest, and no doubt our local fishermen feel some satisfaction that their type of boat, which the experience of generations has evolved, should be chosen as being the best for another part of the British Empire. That the Falkland Islands should have a boat tested by a famous lifeboat hero, Coxswain Henry Blogg, is sufficient guarantee of the seaworthiness of the boat, and should also be of sentimental interest to British people in that far-off island.

There follows a description of the Falkland Islands, then the column ends with:

In 1914 the Governor of the Islands was Sir William Allardyce—who recently retired from the Governorship of Newfoundland. He has visited Sheringham during the past few years, and would doubtless be interested to know that a Sheringham-built boat is now on its way to the Falklands.

The Motor Boat magazine of October 5th, 1928 carried this brief article:

Motor Boat for the Falkland Isles.

An open launch measuring 19 ft. in length has just been completed by Mr. R. Emery, of Sheringham, for shipment to Port Stephens, in the Falkland Islands. This boat, which is of similar design to the local fishing craft, was ordered for the Falkland Islands Co. by a visitor to Cromer, whose experience with the local type of craft indicated that this kind of boat would be ideal for use in the Falkland Isles. The boat, which has a beam of 6 ft. 10½ ins., is fitted with a Brooke motor.

FROM NORTH NORFOLK TO THE FALKLAND ISLANDS.

THE ABOVE MOTOR BOAT WAS MADE BY MR. EMERY, OF SHERINGHAM, AND THE CARRIAGE BY MR. E. ROGERS, OF CROMER. THEY WERE SENT ON FRIDAY TO A PRIVATE COMPANY AT THE FALKLAND ISLANDS.

From the *Norfolk News and People's Weekly Press*:

Saturday, September 15th, 1928. Location Cromer Beach Station.

The vessel was used to ferry shepherds between islands.

Whelk Coppers

A pleasure boat built 1934 for Sir Edward Meyerstein, launched at Sheringham Saturday August 25th, 1934.

Opposite: Sir Edward Meyerstein (right of boat) with *Whelk Coppers* on the day of launch. This photo and the rest, taken by H.H. Tansley from the top workshop, shows a complete mix of people witnessing the occasion. Local and private school children, toffs and many local residents and fishermen are present. Either side of the stem of the vessel can be seen Chris, Marion (their sister) and Harold Emery, then Sir Edward Meyerstein and Robert Emery is far right in his trilby hat. Through the gates at the back can be seen the rear yard of the original *Crown* public house.

Left: A second photo taken from the top workshop.

Top: Robert, Harold and Chris Emery with the new boat and possibly Mr. Davies of Cromer who fitted the engine.

Wealthy Businessman's Eye-Catching Boat and Gifts to the Town

The *Whelk Coppers* is a well-known tea rooms in modern-day Sheringham. But it was also the name of an eye-catching varnished boat built by Robert Emery for a generous businessman, who had made gifts to the community where he made his second home.

Sir Edward Meyerstein, a Jewish merchant, stockbroker and philanthropist, became known as the "Fairy Godfather of Hospitals", due to his generosity in later life by giving £500,000 to London Hospitals. He donated £250,000 to the Middlesex Hospital in London to establish the Meyerstein Institute of Radiotherapy formed in 1936. On one occasion the Middlesex Hospital put up a poster outside the building announcing that £85,675 was needed to complete the new hospital building, Sir Edward bought the poster for the amount shown "as a birthday present to himself," and the reconstruction fund was closed.

Around 1934 Sir Edward purchased the redundant whelk boiling shed on the West Cliff formerly operated by H. R. Johnson. He converted it into a holiday home for his family, naming it *Whelk Coppers* and soon became involved in local life. He bought two new electric winches for the fishermen to replace the hand-operated ones on the east and west beaches—making it much easier to haul the boats up the pebble beach at Sheringham.

Sir Edward also awarded the *Whelk Coppers Cup* and provided the firework display for the annual Sheringham Regatta. Among many other kindly deeds within the community he gave donations to the National Trust to buy land at Roman Camp, West Runton. 1934 was also the year he commissioned the Emerys to build him a motor boat with a special varnished finish.

The following report appeared in the *Eastern Daily Press* of Monday August 27th:

Motor Boat Launched at Sheringham

Built For Mr. E. W. Meyerstein

Considerable interest was shown in the launching at Sheringham on Saturday of a motor boat which had been built for Mr. E. W. Meyerstein, who recently took up residence in the town and is known for his philanthropic interest in the Middlesex Hospital, London. The boat had been built by Sheringham's oldest boatbuilder, Mr. R. Emery, who once built a craft to go to South America. Its dimensions are 16 ft. 8 in. over all, with 6 ft. 5 in. beam and 11 ft. on the keel. Built of larch, it has oak top and sand stroke and oak timbers, and is fitted with a 6 h.p. Stuart engine. It is also fitted for sailing purposes.

The boat bears the same name as Mr. Meyerstein's residence at Sheringham, *Whelk Coppers*. Mr R. Davies, of Cromer fitted the engine. The launching ceremony was carried out by Mrs. Disney, and Mr. Meyerstein and party later made a final trip, which was watched by many people from the beach and sea front.

Sir Edward lived in Sevenoaks, Kent, and was High Sheriff of Kent in 1937–1938 and 1941–1942. In 1886, he married Jessy Louise Solomon. They had two children, a son Edward H. W. Meyerstein, the poet and author, and a daughter Phyllis. He and his wife practised no religion but brought up their two children in the Church of England. Sir Edward died in 1942.

Above left: A happy group of locals and fishermen with the Meyerstein party. Behind Sir Edward can be seen Chris and Harold Emery and to the left of the lady on the front row is their brother Roger, a builder. Above right: Sir Edward Meyerstein at the rear of the old *Crown* pub declares free beer for all—no doubt making him the most popular person present that day.

Below, left: The maiden launch of *Whelk Coppers* from the West Beach. A mixed set of passengers with Chris Emery at the stern ready to put the tiller in place. Centre: Billy 'Cutty' Craske carries a lady passenger back to shore following a successful trip, adding excitement to the occasion. Right: At sea being put through her paces.

Emery Boat-building Skill Immortalised in National Science Museum—in Miniature

A model of a Sheringham crab boat is stored in London's famous Science Museum—thanks to the craftsmanship of Robert Emery … and a fiver's worth of alcoholic "encouragement."

It was created for the British Fishing Boats Exhibition in the summer of 1936, which included a section made up of models and plans of craft from all around the country to capture them for posterity. Most of the models had been acquired by the museum during the inter-war years, but some had originated from the International Fisheries Exhibition of 1883, the London event that, coincidentally, Lewis Emery had exhibited at and is mentioned elsewhere in this book.

Robert's model as originally presented in the Science Museum's British Small Craft display.

At that time the museum was under the directorship of Colonel E. E. Mackintosh and the curator was Geoffrey Swinford Laird Clowes. The model was commissioned through Major Philip Hamond of Scaldbeck House, Morston. Major Hamond was a churchwarden at Stiffkey at the time of the notorious Reverend Harold Davidson, and played a prominent role in the downfall and eventual defrocking of the self-styled Prostitute's Padre in 1932 after he was found guilty of immoral conduct by a church court.

A letter dated 15th October 1934 from Colonel Mackintosh to Major Hamond spelled out his gratitude for the model and the reason for doing it, namely, "to get models of all our coastal small craft, while they still exist and accurate models can be made." Other letters from Mackintosh in November that year enclosed £5, by way of encouragement for Robert Emery, and reveals it was used to pay for pints of ale.

A letter of February 13th, 1935 finds Laird Clowes asking Major Hamond for an update on "how Curly (Robert) Emery is getting on with his model and with the beer." He adds: "We very much hope that the beer is adding strength and accuracy to his hand." The beer must have helped because, after some delays, the completed model was brought to the museum at a cost of £10 paid to Major Hamond and Mr Emery and was officially added to the collection on May 13th, 1935.

A direct letter to Mr Emery dated 24th May, 1935 from Colonel Mackintosh showed his appreciation: "I want to thank you personally for the obvious loving care and first class workmanship which you have put into the model—it is an excellent and delightful piece of work. Now that the model is safe in the National Collections for all time, I hope it will give you comfort and satisfaction to feel that your handiwork will show future generations what Sheringham Crabbers were like, long after the boats have perhaps disappeared or been altered out of all recognition."

Forward in time to 1963 and a new curator, William Thomas O'Dea, had the idea to set up a Sailing Ships Gallery, part of which would be the British Small Craft Display, many of which were displayed in landscape settings.

The Sheringham model was displayed on a beach setting with five fishermen figures carrying the boat with oars through the 'orruck' holes. This display lasted until its removal in late 2012. The model is currently in store.

ACE LN27 (Alice, Clarence, Ernie)

A 24 ft. whelker built 1934 for Ernie 'Blucher' Jarvis, Wells-next-the-Sea.

After twenty years of service with Ernie, in 1955 *ACE* was purchased by Cromer fishermen Robert and Henry 'Shrimp' Davies. She was used in the post-war revival of herring fishing, resulting from a better market for selling the fish after a previous downturn in sales. The vessel was based at Gorleston and, because the whelkers had a forward cuddy, Bob and 'Shrimp' were able to live on her there. Unfortunately the experience was short-lived due to a fire on board. *ACE* had further spells in Wells, Gorleston, and Wells again, before eventually being broken up.

Right: *ACE* emerges from the top workshop ready to go by road to Wells.

Below: *ACE* having arrived from Sheringham parked near the Quay at the bottom of Standard Road.

Left: *ACE* in full sail with 'Diddy' Cooper, Rolly Grimes and Ernie Jarvis.

Blanche LN37

29 ft. whelker built 1937 for 'Titch' and 'Dano' Pegg, Wells-next-the-Sea.

Blanche was later worked by John Nudds at Wells but left the port for the Humber around 1974. Her whereabouts are now unknown.

Right: *Blanche* during her time working from Wells.

Skiff

A newly built skiff in the top workshop with Reginald's daughters: Alice Sadd, with son Colin and Marion Barwick, with son Brian. Reginald and Priscilla had another daughter Mabel who sadly died at the age of four in 1915, following a fall from the promenade on to the beach.

Right: All aboard for adventure in the top workshop.

Rose LN76

Whelker built 1937 for Cyril Grimes, Wells-next-the-Sea.

Rose was launched on Saturday July 3rd, 1937 and towed by car from the workshops down Beach Road to the beach. She was later briefly re-named *Don* then back to *Rose*. Her last years were spent converted into a house-boat and moored in the Stiffkey Freshes before being burned.

Right: *Rose* in her later life as a house boat seen here moored at the Stiffkey Freshes on March 11th, 1984.

Rose on the *Crown* car park, left to right: Reginald Emery, ?, Chris Emery and Harold Emery.

Knot LN95 (Named after the seabird of that name)

A 26 ft. sailing and trawling vessel, built 1938 for Gerald Bullard, Morston.

1938 saw two vessels being constructed in the Lifeboat Plain workshops. *Isabel*, a whelker, was on the bottom workshop stocks having been ordered by fisherman Cyril Loose of Brancaster Staithe. On the upper floor was *Knot*, a 26 ft. pleasure boat being built to the order of Gerald Bullard of Norwich, who ran the family's famous brewery business located at Anchor Brewery off Westwick Street in the city. He wanted a boat that he could use for pleasure and for trawling to be based at Morston.

Two articles appeared in the local paper concerning Knot.

From the *Norfolk Chronicle* Friday May 20th, 1938:

Sheringham Paragraphs

Specially Built

Many have been interested admirers of the large motor boat which has been standing on the *Crown Inn* car park this week. Built by Messrs. Emery, an old firm of local boat builders, it is the largest craft they have ever turned out of the workshop on Lifeboat Plain, whence it was land—'Launched' on Saturday. Estimated to weigh over a ton, it is 26 ft. 3 ins. long, with a beam of 10 ft. It is built of English Oak timbers, Larch planks and Spruce decking, and has a cabin to sleep three persons. It was to leave Sheringham yesterday by road to Morston, where it is to be fitted by Mr W. Temple with a 40 h.p. engine which will enable it to travel at a speed of about nine knots. The boat is also fitted for sailing, and its owner, Mr Gerald Bullard, of Norwich for whom it was specially built, intends to use it for pleasure cruising and trawling purposes.

From *The Norfolk Chronicle* Friday 8th July, 1938:

Morston—A Launching

On Saturday evening the *Knot*, Mr Gerald Bullard's new auxiliary sailing cruiser, was launched at Morston, and was christened by Miss Gene Bullard. On the first trip Mr Bullard was accompanied by the builder, Mr R.E. Emery; the engineer, Mr Temple and 34 others. The vessel, which is fitted with a 40 h.p. engine, has an overall length, including bowsprit, of 33 ft., and a beam of 9 ft. 10 ins. She was built of English Oak at Sheringham by Messrs. Emery. The *Knot* was later handed over to Mr Bullard as "Entirely Satisfactory".

The vessel was actually fitted with a 20 h.p. engine so the speed of nine knots was an exaggeration.

Robert and his two grandsons, Harold and Chris, had gone to Morston to fit out the *Knot* when Robert went missing after a session in the *Anchor* inn where they were boarding. He was eventually found wandering on Morston marshes with the tide coming in, the worse for wear.

Gerald only had the use of *Knot* for a couple of years before the outbreak of the Second World War. He was called up and spent the rest of the war on active service. Gerald had misgivings about keeping a perfectly good boat in store until his return and felt it should be earning a living. *Knot* was sold via Bob Bayfield to 'Diddy' Cooper and the vessel was used for whelking at Wells from 1942 until the mid-70s when she was worked by 'Bouncy' Claxton.

Knot also spent some time working from Great Yarmouth, finally retiring in 2001 to Blakeney Harbour. Eventually around 2008 she was purchased by Gerald's son-in-law Henry Faire and so returned to the ownership of the Bullard family once again.

Gerald had a further two *Knot*s built in the years after the war both built by the Worfolk brothers at King's Lynn.

Thankfully Gerald commissioned local photographer Harry Hodges Tansley to take a series of photos during the different stages of construction of *Knot*. This set of photos is treasured by the Emery family and over the next few pages you can study them closely due to their excellent clarity.

Isabel in the bottom workshop and *Knot* in the top workshop with, left to right, Fisherman Henry 'Deaf Mink' Middleton, Robert, Chris, Harold and Reginald Emery.

The boat takes shape with planks propped up with shores to keep the shape. Chris Emery is seen by the window.

Another view which shows similarity with the construction of Viking longships, a term often used when describing Emery-built boats.

From the rear of the top workshop with the sternpost taking shape. The hole drilled through ready for the prop shaft to be fitted, followed by the propeller.

Wooden tongs holding the planks together with Harold Emery looking on.

Gerald's sister Gene inspects progress on the new vessel.

The curved knees of the thwarts (seats) seen here are made fast to the sides of the boat to hold it all together.

Roof planks in place ready to build the forward cuddy and the forward thwart in place.

Towards the end of the main part of construction.

And from the front of the upper workshop.

Construction in the workshop almost complete. Fitting out would take place later, outside the workshop and at Morston.

Isabel and *Knot* both nearing completion, with Chris and Harold Emery.

Opposite, top left: Saturday May 14th, 1938 and the ramp is built up to the top workshop ready to bring *Knot* down: Gerald Bullard surveying the scene at the top of the ramp on the right. Opposite, top right: The precariously built ramp with Chris and Reginald Emery in the foreground. Opposite, bottom right: The occasion has drawn a number of onlookers including local children unaware of the danger if anything were to go wrong. A case of many hands make light work. Above, left and right: Reginald Emery gives a steadying hand to the emerging vessel. Right: All hands to the rope as the boat slowly eases down the ramp and onto Lifeboat Plain.

Left: Safely on the *Crown* car park ready to go by road to Morston the following day. Below: In front of the new *Crown* public house Gerald Bullard provides free beer for the gathered helpers, plus a few other locals that just happened to be around no doubt.

Time for a family portrait with three generations of the Emery family. Left to right—Robert, Reginald, Harold, Sidney, Jimmy Lewis and Chris with *Knot* on the *Crown* public house car park.

Isabel LN114

A 26 ft. whelker, built in 1938 for Cyril Loose at Brancaster Staithe.

The whelker *Isabel* was built for the Brancaster Staithe fisherman Cyril Loose and named after his wife. Launched from Sheringham beach on Wednesday July 6th, 1938, *Isabel* had a length of 26 ft. 6 ins., a beam of 9 ft. 10 ins. and depth of 4 ft. 5 ½ ins. Planking was larch, while the top strake, keel, stem and stern posts were English oak. As well as being fitted with an Atlantic engine of 16–18 h.p., there was also an Austin Seven car engine to power a hauler. Cyril originally ordered a 30 ft. vessel, but his father, Ernest told his son that 30 ft. would be too big for him to work, especially as they were still hand-hauling. So Cyril went back to the Emery's and asked them to cut 4 ft. off the keel. When he later visited the workshops to see progress, the 4 ft. section was standing in the corner and he always regretted listening to his father.

Cyril was very pleased with *Isabel* and she remained in his ownership until the 1970s, later acting as a reserve boat mainly being used in the winter months. *Isabel* was eventually sold on and ended up derelict in Southwold. She was purchased by Rupert Barclay and brought back to north Norfolk where he and David Hewitt restored her back to working condition. Forward in time and *Isabel* was sold again and the new owner commissioned Daniel Loose, grandson of a cousin of Cyril's, to sympathetically restore the vessel. So in 2013 *Isabel* was launched once again in the presence of Cyril's 90-year-old brother, Ernie Loose. Recently *Isabel* has changed hands again and doesn't give any signs of retiring just yet.

Top: Cyril's sister Catherine with the new boat outside the Lifeboat Plain workshops.

Centre: Catherine and her future mother-in-law, Mrs Elizabeth Southerland. Both photos taken at one of their Sunday visits to see progress with the build.

Bottom: *Isabel* is launched from Sheringham's East Beach using a quant.

Opposite: Cyril Loose at the tiller with Billy Nudds steaming along with a boat load of whelk pots. The photo dates from around 1940.

Sally LN141

A 28 ft. whelker, built 1939/40 for Jimmy Shrum, Wells-next-the-Sea.

Following completion, the *Sally* was taken by train to Wells and put into store for the duration of the Second World War. After the War *Sally* was used for whelking from 1945 up until the mid-1970s including by Tony Jordan, the well-known Wells fisherman. *Sally* remains in Wells under the ownership of Ben Riches.

Sally was actually fitted with a six cylinder Morris Commodore petrol engine, rather than the Gains as in the article printed opposite..

The following article appeared in the local paper during the time that *Sally* was on the stocks.

Tony Jordan and *Sally* at Wells harbour, 1963.

Sally superbly restored by owner Ben Riches and moored at Wells Harbour, January 29th, 2019.

From the *Norfolk Chronicle* Friday September 1st, 1939:

Where Lifeboat was Built

A Sheringham Craftsman

We print this week a picture of Mr. Robert Emery, the well-known Sheringham and North Norfolk boat-builder outside his sheds, where the Sheringham lifeboat *Henry Ramey Upcher* was constructed. The excellent navigability of this boat and her sea-worthiness are by-words among Sheringham lifeboat men, and were recalled at the recent centenary celebrations of the Sheringham lifeboat station. Launched in October, 1894, the *Ramey* was the means of rescuing 202 lives.

In the lifeboat pamphlet it says of this boat, "she was built on the lines of the local fishing boats, and although a hard boat to row, is a very steady and safe boat and is a particularly good boat under sail," and further, "after nearly 42 years' service the *Henry Ramey Upcher* is still in very fair condition".

If you go into the building sheds you can see the skeleton of a whelker which Mr. Emery, his son Reginald, and grandsons, Harold and Chris, are engaged in making. When ready it will be the largest boat of its kind made by the Emery family. It is 28 feet in length and its beam is 10 feet. Clinker-built, its stem and stern posts are made of oak and the body of the boat is of larch wood. It will be powered by a 50 h.p. Gains Universal engine. From start to finish it will probably take four months to construct this whelker, which will be in service off Wells, where several boats now employed in the same trade were made in the same boat-yard.

CRABS AND LOBSTERS

NORFOLK COAST PERSONALITIES

MR. ROBERT EMERY, Sheringham.

59

Passing of 'Curly'

From the *North Norfolk News* October 18th, 1941:

Passing of 'Curly' Emery, Noted Sheringham Boatbuilder

From a Special Correspondent

Along the East Coast there was no character more highly esteemed and beloved than Robert (Curly) Emery, of Sheringham boatbuilder and saviour of human lives, who has just died at the age of 77. Thanks to his native intelligence, his skill as a craftsman and his intimate knowledge of the difficulties and perils of the North Sea, the boats which he built at his yard on Lifeboat Plain were in constant demand from Flamborough Head to Whitstable, and on one never-to-be-forgotten occasion a boat of his making was once chosen for service in the Falkland Islands.

A double-ended crab boat on Sheringham beach with Robert Emery far left.

Beautiful Starnpost

To him belonged the honour of being the first man to fit an engine into a Norfolk crab boat. To the layman this may seem a simple enough operation, but it is actually nothing of the kind. An East Anglian boat needs many alterations and adaptations before it can be used for such a purpose, not the least important of these being the sternpost. 'Curly' designed and perfected one which is universally admitted to be "a beautiful starnpost."

Built First Lifeboat

He also had the distinction of having designed and built the first (privately owned) lifeboat in these parts. It was constructed largely at the personal cost of the then squire, of timber cut from his woods and was named after his grandfather Henry Ramey Upcher. She did service for very many years till she was replaced by a National Institution boat. She is now spending the twilight of her life in her old home on Lifeboat Gangway, but she still comes out of retirement occasionally in case of emergency.

Quick Thinking

One of 'Curly's' best-remembered adventures in her took place at the wreck of the *Commodore* a good many years ago. The vessel had run ashore in a fog, but a heavy gale arose and hurled the lifeboat against her side, stoving in some planks. Here 'Curly's' ready wits came to work. With such material as was handy, he made shift to patch up the leaks while the crew was actually being lowered into the lifeboat and, by the time they were all aboard, she was in a fit condition to take them safely ashore. 'Curly's' long life was well spent. He will be greatly missed, but his memory will last on as long as lifeboat-men and fisherfolk have tales to tell about the sea.

The funeral took place at St. Peter's Church on Wednesday, the Rev J. F. Grattan Guiness officiating. The mourners included Mr. and Mrs. Reggie Emery, Mr. J. L. Emery, Mr. R. W. Emery, Mr. and Mrs. C. Emery, Mrs Elizabeth Emery, Mrs R. W. Cox, Miss M. Emery, Mr. Robert Emery and Mrs H. Emery.

Enterprise YH201

A 19 ft crab boat, built 1945 for Sidney 'Plug' Emery, Sheringham.

Following the Second World War, the first new boat to emerge from the workshops was for Reginald's youngest son, Sidney. Sidney sent word home to his father and two brothers to start building his boat ready for when he arrived back from service in the Royal Navy.

The boat was in use up until the early 1960s when 'Plug' changed career to working in antiques and creating nautical displays for films, television and shop windows in London. The opening fishing village scenes in the 1967 film of *Doctor Dolittle* contains crab pots, fishing nets and peds (wicker baskets used for storing crabs in the boat) originally from Sheringham provided by Sidney. He also set the main entrance display for the International Boat Show at Earl's Court for over a decade.

Enterprise is now in Sheringham Museum.

Right: Sidney Emery with his new boat on Sheringham's East Beach.

Above: After returning home from a fishing trip with son Malcolm 'Young Plug' and veteran fisherman 'Loady' West.

Below: Norfolk maritime historian Robert Malster looks over *Enterprise* at Sheringham Museum.

Left: Extra income could be made during the summer months from taking visitors out to sea for trips. Here Sidney is seen with lifelong friend fisherman Henry 'Joyful' West. In fact Sidney met his future wife Betty on one of these occasions.

Lewis James YH210

A 19 ft. 6 ins. crab boat, built in 1947 for Lewis 'Tuna' Harrison, Cromer.

After the end of the Second World War in 1945, the government made available loans or grants to fishermen to use for the purchase of gear or towards a boat, to help revive the fishing industry. One of the first boats to be built by grant aid was for Lewis 'Tuna' Harrison of Cromer. 'Tuna' was a relation of the Emerys, his grandmother Elizabeth being the daughter of Lewis 'Buffalo' Emery. As the boat was being part paid by the government, a proper contract was required to be drawn up by a solicitor.

'Tuna' later said that he was glad of the contract as he knew his boat would be ready by a certain date. The Emerys had a reputation, as did many businesses in those more laid back times, for taking time to complete a boat especially as there were several in construction following the war.

Later, after 'Tuna' had retired, *Lewis James* was purchased by the Scotter family and renamed *Peter James* and worked from Sheringham, before eventually being broken up.

Peter James (*Lewis James*) in her last years stored at the Hewitt Brothers' boatyard in Blakeney on September 23rd, 1981.

KP&K YH76 (Kathleen, Patricia & Kitty)

A 19 ft. 11ins. crab boat built in 1947 for Henry 'Shrimp' Davies, Cromer.

KP&K was regarded by many fisherman as the best crab boat of her generation. She was used by renowned local seafarer 'Shrimp' Davies who was well-known and respected both as a fisherman and lifeboat coxswain. He knew a good boat when he saw one.

When Sheringham boat-building ceased in 1957, the fishermen turned to the Norfolk Broads, and in particular to Maycraft at Potter Heigham. The firm was owned by Billy May and his first crab boat was built in 1959 for Dennis Gaff of Cromer. Named *William Robert*, measurements were taken of *KP&K* to help with the construction of Billy's first attempt at a crab boat. The boat was a success and Billy went on to build many more for the local fishermen over the next 26 years before retirement.

Above: Having been taken by road from Sheringham, the new boat is seen here in the workshops of East Coast Motor Company in Church Street, Cromer where their mechanic Joe Linder is installing the new Parsons engine. With him are Harold Emery left and Henry 'Shrimp' Davies on the right.

Left: *KP&K* steaming through Blakeney with David Hewitt at the tiller.

William Edward LN8

Built 1949 for Cyril 'Gully' Grimes, Wells-next-the-Sea, she was the largest whelker to be built by the Emerys. The latter part of construction took place outside the workshops.

Length: 30 ft., width: (amidships) 10 ft. 9 ins., depth: 4 ft. 8 ins.

She weighed 6 tons and took 10 months to construct.

Opposite: 'Too-fee' Farrow and Reginald Emery with *William Edward* nearing the stage where the vessel would have to be moved outside the workshops for completion. Top Right: *William Edward* has been moved onto the car park of the *Windham Arms* public house next door (see also page 17) to complete the fitting out and to install the motor and hauler as the workshop ceiling height made it impossible to carry on working on a boat this size. Below: Moving the boat from the workshops past the *Crown* on the left. In the foreground is a skeet which is a wooden frame with two free-running cast iron rollers that the keel of the boat can move over. Right centre: Moving past the *Bijou Hotel* (now the *Two Lifeboats*) on the left with anyone that is available hauling on the rope, including local children. Right bottom: Reginald can be seen in the centre with three fishermen carrying one of the large skeets borrowed from the *Henry Ramey Upcher* lifeboat shed. *William Edward* was four feet shorter and only seven inches narrower than the lifeboat so the skeets were an ideal size.

Top left: Easing past *The Lobster* ready to move down Wyndham Street. Above: At the bottom of Beach Road on the fishermen's slipway. Centre left: A good indication of the amount of people that were involved with the move as well as those who turned out to watch. Bottom left: Slowly and carefully edging the boat over the shingle beach towards the sea. Below: Finally preparing to sail on her maiden voyage to Wells. All the time the sea is getting rougher.

From the *North Norfolk News* 3rd December, 1948:

Sheringham Crab-Boat Builders

Henry Upcher Lifeboat was their Work

Mr Reginald Emery and his two sons, Messrs. Harold and Chris Emery, are among the last of the crab-boat builders to remain active on the North Norfolk coast. The business, housed in a small double-storeyed workshop, is tucked away in Gun Street, Sheringham. Two boats can be built at the same time; one upstairs and one down. The engines can be fitted only when the boats are removed from the shops into the open yard, because there is insufficient headroom in the shops. The boat occupying the upper-story stocks has to be removed through the open end of the upper shop by means of a sloping platform, down which it slides.

The Emery business began about 100 years ago in a perhaps unusual fashion. The founder was Mr. Lewis (Buffalo) Emery, the present senior Mr. Emery's grandfather. He was a fisherman and he needed a new boat. No one could be found to build it for him. Mr. Emery, a practical man, decided on the only solution—to build it himself. He did so and because of its success he found such a ready trade in boat-building on the north Norfolk coast and in Lincolnshire, too, that he forsook the sea and set up business. Since then son has followed father for four generations.

Saved Over 200

The majority of crab boats at Cromer and Sheringham have been made by the Emery family. Their work has gone as far afield as the Falkland Islands. But of all the craft which have been built in their small shop the most famous was the former Sheringham lifeboat, the *Henry Ramey Upcher*, which saved 202 lives at sea in her 56 years' service.

She is in her shed to this day, and when the *Monte Nuria*, the Spanish cargo vessel, ran aground at Sheringham earlier this year and the RNLI lifeboat *Foresters' Centenary*, was unavailable, the lifeboat crew almost decided to launch this old stalwart to go to the steamer's assistance.

A crab boat, as any visitor to the workshop can see, is made of the finest woods available. Larch is used for the planking, oak for the ribs and keel, and it has to possess grain, running in the direction of the bends. The craft is known as boat-building, but some formal word would seem to be needed to suggest a sense of growth, as of a living thing. There are no blue-prints, no plans, and no machine tools are employed. Says Mr. Emery, sen.: "We use our eye and that's how they are built. People are often amazed when I tell them that this is how we construct a boat." Mr. Emery explains that in his method of boat-building the boat is actually built to shape and the ribs put in afterwards. The ribs are usually inserted first in most forms of construction.

Began Early

Ruminating on his craft, he says: "You've got to be brought up in it from childhood. I started working in this shop when I was eleven." One of his sons added that he and his brother used to go to the shop after school most days. That was how they began their apprenticeship.

A testimony to the family skill reposes in the Science Museum at South Kensington. It is a model crab boat made by the late Mr. Robert Emery, father of the present owner. *William Edward* was launched on Monday 25th April 1949 which prompted the following article:

From the *North Norfolk News* Friday 29th April, 1949:

Launching of the *William Edward*

Largest Whelk Boat Made in Sheringham

Hundreds of Sheringham people gathered at the Beach Road entrance to the sea on Monday to watch the largest whelk boat, *William Edward*, made by Mr. Reginald Emery and his two sons in their small boat-building shop at Sheringham, launched for her maiden trip to Wells.

Weighing nearly six tons this boat was man-handled from the workshop in Gun Street, through the Council car park on the front, along High Street, Wyndham Street and finally to the beach. The operation took nearly two hours. There was no champagne used at this launching, but it was an event which captured the imagination of Sheringham for men, women and children lined the roads and the promenade to watch her slip into the water. In addition to the crew several local people sailed in her to Wells where she will be used by her owner, Mr. C. Grimes, a Wells fisherman.

The boat has taken Mr. Emery and his sons 10 months to build. She is 30 ft. long, 10 ft. 9 in. wide amidships and 4 ft. 8 in. deep. No blueprints were necessary in her construction. "We use our eye, that's how she is made," said Mr. Emery, whose grandfather established the business about 100 years ago.

As the boat slipped into the water, the crowd watched her roll, ship a little sea which soaked one of the passengers, then raise her head majestically to meet the next wave. She was afloat and the crowd gave her a cheer. A brief cruise on the foreshore was all that was necessary to reassure the craftsmen who built her that their work was sound. The boat's crew waved their handkerchiefs, the crowd cheered again and the *William Edward* put her nose westwards towards Wells.

The photo of *William Edward* in construction, with a colourised version used on the cover of this book, was taken by a Leicester photographer for an article in the local paper.

Memories—*William Edward*

Michael Emery   March 2021

Schoolboy memories of the maiden trip of *William Edward*.

The *William Edward* was a whelk boat built by my grandfather, father and uncle in 1948–49. She was the largest boat built in the Lifeboat Plain workshop at 30 ft. long. The boat was built for Cyril Grimes of Wells at a cost of £850.00, not including the engine.

The keel was laid in September–October of 1948. She was launched in April 1949, having been hauled from Lifeboat Plain, past the *Crown Inn*, up past the *Seaview Hotel*, then past the *Bijou Hotel* (now the *Two Lifeboats*), down Wyndham Street then down Beach Road, after a bit of juggling at the junction, then down to the east beach. This was done by manpower with schoolboys hauling on ropes and the boat being moved on skeets. There was no traffic in those days. You could never attempt this today!

Once on the east beach the boat was made ready to launch. It was not a nice day, with a stiff breeze blowing, making the sea very choppy. I was determined to be in the boat for its first trip. My father tried to put me off saying the sea was too rough, but I still went with my brother Richard and my mother and father and Uncle Sidney. There were others whom I cannot remember (I was only nine at the time), but there were about a dozen in the boat.

We all got in and the boat was launched. We were bouncing about from the start. I should have listened to my father. I remember someone saying, "We are just passing the lifeboat shed". Apart from being sick over the side that was the last thing I remember about the trip. We were put in the cuddy hole at the front of the boat and I passed out.

The next thing I recall is being lifted out at Wells Harbour and being laid down to recover. As luck would have it a Sheringham builder, a Mr. Nichols, had driven to Wells to see the boat in and offered us a lift home as amazingly my father had made no arrangements to get us home!

The *William Edward* was worked most of her life by Tony Jordan who was the stepson of Cyril Grimes, and he later told me that he was on that first trip aged 18 years old.

Later in the 1990s Tony retired and sold the *William Edward*. I spotted the advert in the *Eastern Daily Press* and contacted Tony and introduced myself to him. He suggested I come over to Wells the next day as he was going to take the boat from his whelk sheds down to Wells Harbour ready to go to Great Yarmouth. I could also be on its last trip from Wells, which I did. The boat had been fitted with a wheelhouse so looked a lot different to when I first went in her.

Tony suggested that I came with him to take the boat to Great Yarmouth the next day. I declined the offer as the first time was still in my mind. The next day was very breezy so I had made the right choice.

I learnt later on that *William Edward* was finally burnt and Tony is no longer with us. A sad end to a lovely boat and a fond farewell to a lovely man.

William Edward was the last wooden whelker to work from the port of Wells. However before the boat's demise, David Hewitt took a mould of the hull from which a GRP boat was produced and named *Blucher*. She was worked from Wells by Andy McCallum until being taken over by Ben Gathercole. So you could say that the ghost of *William Edward* lives on.

Our Boys YH35

A 19 ft. 11 ins. crab boat built 1950 for Bob 'Joyful' West, Sheringham

Our Boys had a long spell working from Sheringham with Bob 'Joyful' and his two sons, Henry 'Joyful' and Jack 'Jacko'. They later inherited the boat following their father's death and continued to work her from the East Beach at Sheringham.

Bob's son Henry 'Joyful' recalled:

> After the war, the Emerys were very busy with orders for whelk boats as well as crabbers. Father's boat was laid down in the upper storey in early 1949. At that time the Emerys were working on a whelk boat on the ground floor. This was the 30 ft. *William Edward* which was the largest whelk boat built in Sheringham, and so the final painting and fitting out had to be completed outside. I and brother Jack tarred the lower hull of *William Edward* so that the Emerys could be freed up to work on father's boat.

Neither of Henry and Jack's sons pursued a career in fishing, so on their retirement *Our Boys* was sold to Rupert Barclay in 1994, then fully restored and maintained by him and David Hewitt from then on. He sold her to a private owner and she was used as a pleasure boat. Eventually the boat came up for sale and Henry's son Robin jumped at the chance and bought her back into the family in 2017. And so another chapter began for *Our Boys*.

Top left: *Our Boys* on Sheringham's East Beach around 1981. Top right: Linda and Robin West proudly stand alongside *Our Boys* at Wells Tugboat Yard, Saturday July 28th, 2018. Centre right: *Our Boys* beaches for winching, August 11th, 1982. Bottom left: Henry 'Joyful' West brings home the catch. Bottom right: Brother 'Jacko' West looks over the gunwale.

Harvester LN105

A 26 ft. whelker, built 1951 for Sid 'Custard' Cooper, Wells-next-the-Sea.

This was the last whelker to be built by the Emerys. She was launched on Saturday June 30th, 1951. Sid worked *Harvester* up until 1971 when she then spent time at Blakeney and Thornham. She also had a spell taking out fishing parties to earn her keep.

From the *Eastern Daily Press* Monday 2nd July, 1951:

Maiden Voyage of a Whelk Boat

A new whelk boat, *Harvester*, 26 ft. long, made her maiden voyage to Wells on Saturday. Among those who made the trip from Sheringham were Mr. C. F. Mills, vice-chairman of Sheringham U.D.C (Urban District Council), and Mr. J. E. Bell a member of the council. With them also were two old Sheringham fishermen, Mr. Abraham Cooper, aged 93, and Mr. P. Wilson, ten years his junior. The *Harvester* is the second large whelk boat turned out by the Emery family of craftsmen at their Sheringham workshop since the war. A refinement in the new boat is a hydraulic winch for hauling. The craft has taken about two years to build.

Above: *Harvester* restored and moored at Wells Tugboat Yard in October 2019, under the ownership of Rescue Wooden Boats based at Stiffkey.

Top: Reginald Emery with his son Sidney 'Plug' and grandson Malcolm 'Young Plug' in Beach Road with *Harvester* before its maiden trip. Centre: The boat is moved carefully down over the pebble beach. Bottom: Waiting on the East Beach for the incoming tide. At the tiller is former fisherman Abraham Cooper who had come out of retirement for the occasion. Sadly he passed away a few months later, aged 94.

Windsor Rose YH192

A 19 ft. 6 ins. crab boat built 1952/53 for Jimmy Scotter, Sheringham.

Windsor Rose had a long career at Sheringham being used by Jimmy and his son Arthur, then Arthur and his son Peter, before being placed on permanent loan to Sheringham Museum where she was preserved and is on display.

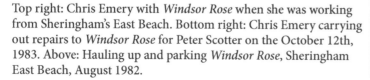

Top right: Chris Emery with *Windsor Rose* when she was working from Sheringham's East Beach. Bottom right: Chris Emery carrying out repairs to *Windsor Rose* for Peter Scotter on the October 12th, 1983. Above: Hauling up and parking *Windsor Rose*, Sheringham East Beach, August 1982.

Black Beauty YH347

A 19 ft. 10 ins. crab boat built 1952 for Jack Davies, Cromer.

From the *Eastern Daily Press* May 2nd, 1952:

New Crab Boat Brought Downstairs

A new crab boat, built by Mr. R. Emery at Lifeboat Plain, Sheringham, was brought downstairs last evening from the loft in which it had been constructed. In the downstairs workshop, an engine will be fitted into the still-empty hull of *Black Beauty*, which has been built for a Cromer fisherman, Mr. J. J. Davies, formerly second coxswain of the Cromer lifeboat.

A ramp of heavy baulks of timber was made from the loft to the ground. Then, with eight men below to haul her down and others at the back to prevent her from running away or tilting, the boat was lowered.

Mr. Emery has built most of the crab boats used at Cromer. The last one was for a nephew of the owner of the boat which was brought downstairs last night.

Black Beauty was later used by Andy and Martin Frary at Wells before being donated to Rescue Wooden Boats for their collection at Stiffkey.

Top right: *Black Beauty* moored in Wells harbour during the time she was used by the Frary brothers. Centre right: *Black Beauty* at Bayfield Hall near Holt in August 2016 under the ownership of Rescue Wooden Boats and awaiting restoration. Bottom left: Tending herring nets, Cromer East Beach, c. 1959. Bottom right: Roy Cork drives the tractor to pull *Black Beauty* back up the beach at Cromer in the 1970s.

The Day the Nation Listened to the Emery Boat-building Story

"Good evening This is the BBC Home Service." It is 7pm on July 15th, 1953.

Reginald Emery's colourful insight into the family boat-building company was broadcast live from Norwich Assembly House during a 30-minute programme called *Down To The Sea*. Alas, we cannot find a recording but we have the next best thing—a transcript of Reginald's words heard on the 'wireless'. Tune in, sit back and enjoy.

Well, if herrings have been caught out of Lowestoft for a thousand years, then it's more than likely we've been catching whelks at Sheringham for just about as long.

At any rate, my family has been building boats for the local fishermen for more than a hundred years and we're still doing so today. About 1870, my grandfather Lewis Emery, had his four sons, James, Robert, Ben and John working with him. And there were other builders at that time—Harry Lown and his nephew, Edward Skipper and Robert and Tom Boxall. Between them, they launched twenty new boats every year.

Now the shape and construction of these boats hasn't altered at all in living memory, and there is no reason why they should, as they are perfectly suited for this part of the coast. They are double-ended, that is pointed at both stem and stern, and are quite open, having no deck of any sort. I have recently built them up to 30 feet for the whelk fishing at Wells and Brancaster but the Cromer and Sheringham men want them about 19 feet.

They have a width of about seven feet and a depth of just over three feet, so they are quite beamy boats and need to be for safety when handling pots in anything of a sea. The only change that has come about in my lifetime is that now they all have engines, where once they had only sails. Then they had one mast, stepped fairly well forward, and secured to the foremost seat with a stout iron clasp. This was the only fixing as they had no shrouds or stays. The mast was about 18 feet high and on this was hoisted a lugsail made of 35 yards of heavy calico or duck, and tanned to a deep brown. You'll get some idea of the size of this when I tell you that the foot of the sail was as long as the boat herself while the yard was about six inches longer. With this amount of canvas, they were powerful boats at sea.

At Sheringham, we are proud of the fact that every boat is hand-made, the only machinery we use being an electric drill. The keel, deadwood, stem and stern posts which come out of best English oak, are cut with an ordinary hand-saw and shaped with an adze. There are eleven planks on either side, made from oak and English larch, ½ an inch thick.

Inside there are 36 timbers, or ribs, 1¾ inches by 1¼ inches, also of oak, which are steamed to shape and fitted after the hull has been planked up. This is done clinker fashion, that is, the bottom edge of the upper plank overlaps the top edge of the one below it, and the ribs are jogged with a drawknife to fit every plank sweetly.

As you may know, the usual way of building boats is to set up three or more moulds, carefully cut to shape, and round these the planks are fitted to make certain of a nice clean run from stem to stern. Really, they act as a template for the whole shape of the hull. Well, some of the old Norfolk wherry builders had such a keen eye that they could build a fifty foot wherry with no more than a single mould amidships, but we've gone one better than that and don't use any moulds at all. We do everything by eye and careful measurement.

The keel, which is 3½ inches square, the stem post which is 2½ inches thick and the stern post which is 3 inches thick, have to be cut out of wood grown to shape. So do the knees and 'wrongs' to get the proper grain for maximum strength. The oak, used for the keel, stem and stern posts, is seasoned for three years before being used and the planks for one year. The larch doesn't need to be seasoned, nor do the timbers, but these must be nice clean wood, free from any knots.

Only copper nails are used for fastenings and galvanised and brass screws as these won't rust. When finished, the bottom is tarred and the topsides painted according to the fancy of the owner, but usually in bands of white, blue, yellow or red.

Even though they have engines, every boat still carries a set of oars as they did in the sailing days. But an interesting thing about this is that there are no rowlocks or thole pins, but holes made in the top strake or plank. In the choppy water off this part of the coast, an oar could very easily jump out of a rowlock with serious results, but this is quite impossible with our arrangement. And in days gone by when, with no harbour, the boats had to be moved up the beach, this was done by putting the oars right through these holes, 'ollocks' as we call them, on either side, the crew getting hold of each end of the oars and carrying them in much the same way as bearers carry a coffin.

They cradled the oar on their forearms, however, instead of having it on their shoulders, but then the Sheringham men were so brawny that it took no more than four of them to walk a boat right up the beach. But you won't see them doing it today with a great engine in, any more than you will see coal carts on the foreshore as we did in my young day.

The coal carts came down to the sailing colliers which beached themselves at high water and then unloaded their coal into them as the tide went down. By the time the tide was up again, they would be discharged and hauling themselves off to go back to Newcastle for another load.

Nearly all my family's work has been building fishing boats, although my father and grandfather between them did build also the sailing and pulling lifeboat which did many years of fine service on the Sheringham station before she was replaced with a more modern boat. But she still lies in her boat house and there has been some talk locally of preserving her. I wish this could happen as she is one of the few surviving examples of this type and would help to remind the generations to come of what the days of sail were like round the Norfolk coast.

Fisherman Jimmy 'Mace' Johnson with Reginald sorting through some 'beautiful bends' as he would say, namely planks that were suitable to cut the curved stem and stern posts from for a boat. The picture was taken by famous photographer Olive Edis in 1944 and has been partly restored due to the condition it was in when found in the workshops.

Miss Corringdon YH7

A 18 ft. crab boat, built 1954 for Mr. J. H. Green, West Runton.

Miss Corringdon was launched on Thursday April 8th, 1954. Her measurements were: length 18 ft. 8 ins., beam 7 ft. 4 ins. and she was fitted with an 8.28 hp. engine. After a long life working from West Runton, the boat was finally broken up.

Right: *Miss Corringdon* is being moved down Beach Road to the sea ready for her maiden voyage to West Runton in 1954.

Left: With the motor started, the boat prepares to sail to West Runton on her maiden trip.

Miss Britain YH56

A 19 ft. crab boat built in 1955 for Jimmy 'Paris' West, Sheringham.

Launched Saturday July 2nd, 1955.

Jimmy previously always had his boats built by one of the other Sheringham boat-builders, Johnny Johnson. But, as John had retired at the end of 1949, Jimmy ordered a new vessel from the Emerys. He later stated that he was happy with the boat and worked her until his retirement.

The naming ceremony was carried out by Jimmy's daughter, Pam, by breaking a bottle of port wine over the bows.

Miss Britain as she is today moored at Tugboat Yard in Wells under new ownership.

Jimmy with his new boat on the day of its maiden trip. Next to him is his daughter Pam.

Stills taken from Brian Coe's film of the launch of *Miss Britain*.

Charles Mark YH39

A 19 ft. crab boat built 1957 for Richard Davies, Overstrand.

This was the last boat to be constructed by the Emery family. Following the death of Reginald's beloved wife Priscilla in January, 1957, Reg lost all interest in anything to do with work and stopped going to the workshops, leaving his son Harold to complete the boat alone. However Reg saw the boat completed but not launched. The launch was to have been from Sheringham on Saturday March 23rd, 1957, but because of high water she was taken by road to Overstrand, where she was finally put in the water five days later. Reginald died in June 1957.

Top: Richard Davies with his new boat at Overstrand in 1957.
Bottom left & right: *Charles Mark* working off Overstrand.

A Dying Craft—Obituaries on the Boat Builders

Reg

From the *North Norfolk News* June 7th, 1957:

Death of a Sheringham Craftsman

Through the death in Cromer Hospital on Monday of Mr. Reginald Edward Emery, of Victoria Street, Sheringham, the district has lost one of the 'old school' of craftsmen in a trade which is fast becoming in this area a trade of a past age—that of boat-building. Mr. Emery, who entered hospital six days earlier, was 74. He was a grandson of Mr. Lewis ("Buffalo") Emery, who founded the boat-building business about 100 years ago. Beginning work at the age of 12, Mr. Emery worked under the supervision of his grandfather for some time. On the latter's death the business was taken over by his father, Mr. Robert Emery. It was at the beginning of the First World War that father and son built the first motor-powered crab boat in the country. Previously they had been constructing sailing crab boats at the rate of about one a month—in the days when there were well over 100 fishing boats in Sheringham. Now the number is about 20, although at one time—about 1935—the total had dropped to as low as 15. In 1896 it is estimated there were some 250 fishing boats in use from Sheringham.

Worked in Shipyards

During the First World War Mr. Emery worked in the ship-building yards of Messrs. Fairfield at Glasgow, constructing ships' lifeboats. In addition to his 63 years as a boat builder, Mr. Emery had also, for the past 35 years, let chairs and tents out to visitors during the summer on the promenade. In this work he had been assisted by his wife, who died in January. In recent years the business has been carried on by Mr. Emery and his son, Harold. The last boat he had worked on was *Charles Mark*, a crab boat ordered by Mr. Richard Davies, of Overstrand, which was launched in April. Mr. Emery was a keen bowls player in his younger days. He leaves five sons and two daughters. Mr. Harold Emery hopes to carry on the business for the present. The funeral service was at St. Peter's Church, Sheringham, yesterday afternoon.

Harold

From the *North Norfolk News* June 7th, 1981:

Sheringham Boatbuilder has Died

Well-known local boatbuilder Mr. Harold Emery, of 25, The Avenue, Sheringham, has died at Papworth Hospital, aged 68. He was the third generation of the family to carry on the trade at Sheringham. His grandfather, the late Mr. Lewis Emery, built the lifeboat *Henry Ramey Upcher* for Mrs. Caroline Upcher, of Sheringham. There were no plans or blueprints for this or any other boat built by the firm. The business was carried on by his son, Mr. Reggie (Calais) [sic] Emery, and after he died Mr. Harold Emery continued the building of fishing boats. He retired two years ago. He leaves a widow and three sons.

Harold and *Isabel*.

Chris

From the *North Norfolk News*, 1987:

End of an era as Chris Emery dies

Sheringham is mourning the death of one of its last links with the town's former boat-building industry. Mourners filled St. Peter's Church on Wednesday for the funeral of 73-year-old Mr Chris Emery, whose family boat-building tradition began more than a century ago.

Mr Emery, of Victoria Street, worked with his brother, Harold, father, Reginald, and grandfather, Robert, in their Lifeboat Plain workshop during the 1920s. The craft he helped to build were renowned the length of the East Coast. He built several of the familiar crab boats used at Sheringham and Cromer and also larger whelkers used at Wells and Brancaster.

Years ago, one of Mr Emery's boats was sent to the Falkland Islands to carry shepherds between islands. After the decline of the boat-building industry, he worked in Norwich. On retirement, Mr Emery continued in the family business of letting beach huts and deck chairs on Sheringham's East Promenade. Mr Emery leaves a widow, Elizabeth.

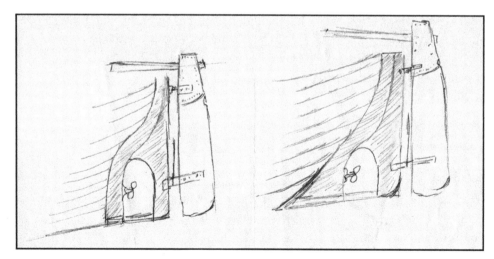

A critical moment—Chris Emery's sketch shows his grandfather Robert's original design for his 'starnpost' to fit motors on the left and a later adaption for the design on the right.

The Emery Family Workshops

Lifeboat Plain, Sheringham

Michael Emery remembers the workshops on Lifeboat Plain, and the following pages feature a series of photos taken after the death of Harold Emery in 1981. They show the building and interior before and during clearance ready for remodelling into two dwellings. He writes in October 2020:

Memories and Smells of Emerys' Boat-building Workshop on Lifeboat Plain, Sheringham 1946–1950

As you walked in through the doors you were aware of the soil floor which had indentations in it. They were where my great-grandfather Robert, grandfather Reginald, father Harold and uncle Chris had worked around the boats, lying underneath when clinkering up (when the ribs or timbers are fixed to the planking).

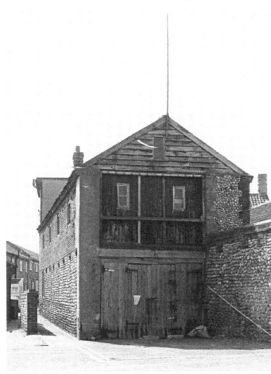

There was a winding staircase to the right leading to upstairs with a door at the top to keep draughts down to a minimum. Also on the ground floor were two sets of stocks so they could build two boats at a time on the ground floor. On the left was a workbench, to the right was a door leading to a yard outside where surplus materials were stored for future use! I also remember a grindstone in the yard for sharpening tools.

You then climbed the winding staircase to upstairs. Very dark it was too, until you opened the door at the top, when you were greeted with the scent of wood—oak and larch—a smell I could recall for years. There would be a boat on the stocks under construction. This would be done by lapping one board over the one below and then ribs fixed to stabilise the boat. All these timbers had to be steamed to get the boat shape. The copper used for the steaming was situated to the right upstairs with a trunking above to feed the timber in with sacking over to help retain the steam. Steaming took about four hours, a very slow process. Every part of the boat-building was done by hand and eye and careful measurement.

Also upstairs were two more sets of stocks so that in busy periods four boats could be built at a time, two downstairs and two upstairs. I personally only remember two boats being built at one time which was in 1949 when a whelk boat, *William Edward*, was on the stocks downstairs bound for Wells, and a crab boat , *Our Boys*, for a Sheringham fisherman upstairs. Any boat built upstairs had to be lowered down a ramp, all done by sheer manpower.

At the rear upstairs were slabs of oak with thin splines between to allow air to circulate in order to dry out the timber. It had to be seasoned timber (deadwood) for the keel, stem and stern posts. There appeared to be a general disorder and untidiness around, but amongst this they produced hundreds of boats over the decades—originally rowing boats and later from the First World War motor boats that went all round the Norfolk coast and beyond.

There also appeared to be lots of cats around, I expect to keep down the vermin.

Top, from the left: Looking from the yard of what was Govan Cottage where the Emery family lived and was brought up. Detail of one of the windows in the passage between the workshops and the *Windham Arms* public house. Each end of the passage between the workshops and the *Windham Arms*. Bottom: Advertising signs for Morris Marine Engines and the rear of the workshop being used to store deck chairs. Right:The lower workshop prior to being cleaned out ready for conversion work.

From top left : One of the work benches, a view to the main doors, Trevor Emery begins clearing piles of wood. Centre from left: Two pictures of benches and tools, progress with clearing and the steamer on the right. Lower two pictures: The stocks where the keel was attached to begin construction of boats. There were two in the top workshop and two in the bottom; at busy times up to four boats could be under construction.

Above: The stairs down to the bottom workshop. The top workshop in earlier times had been the home of Sheringham's first Salvation Army Corps, first using this building on May 3rd, 1888. Many Salvationists would have walked up and down these stairs during the time they were based here.

Above: Some of the many tools used in the construction of the boats laying on the bench which ran full length down the left side of the top workshop. Many of these tools are now on show in Sheringham Museum. Below: The steamer where all the timbers were softened ready for bending into shape, using the process as explained earlier.

Michael Emery secures the top workshop doors for the last time.

Contracts

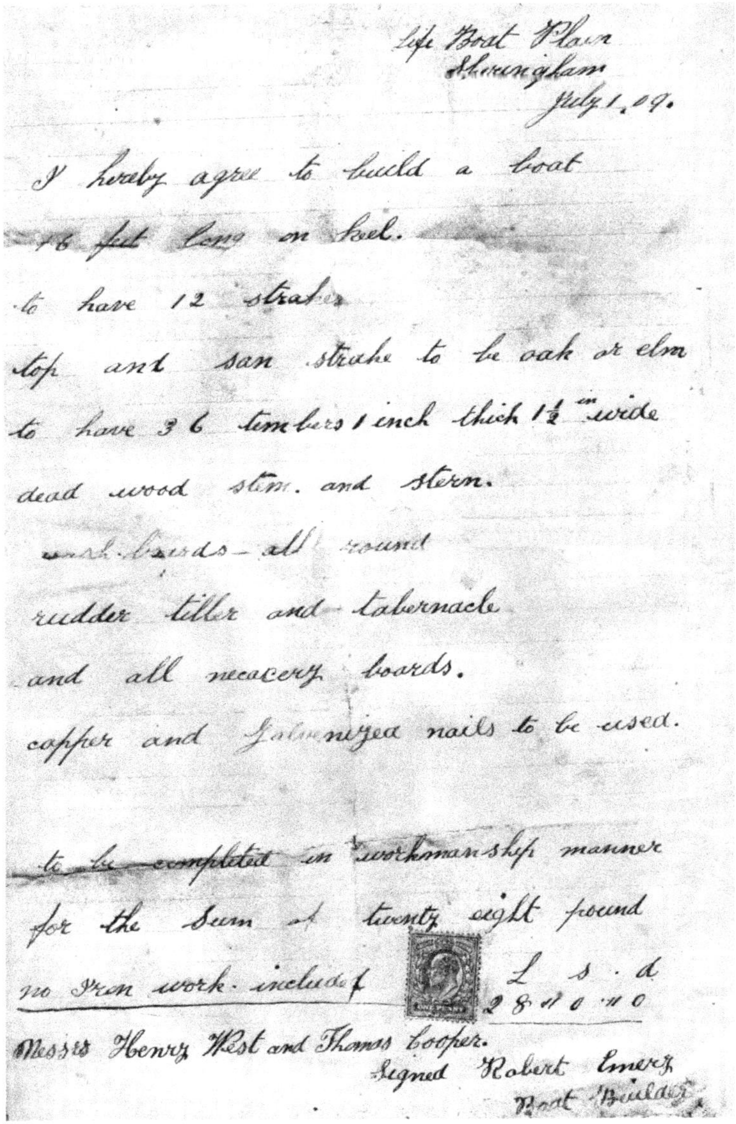

14 Boat Plain
Sheringham
July 1. 09.

I hereby agree to build a boat
16 feet long on keel.

to have 12 strakes

top and san strake to be oak or elm

to have 36 timbers 1 inch thick 1½ in wide

dead wood stem. and stern.

wash boards - all round

rudder tiller and tabernacle

and all necacery boards.

copper and Galvanized nails to be used.

to be completed in workmanship manner

for the sum of twenty eight pound

no iron work. included   £   s . d
                              28 . 0 . 0

Messrs Henry West and Thomas Cooper.

Signed Robert Emery
Boat Builder

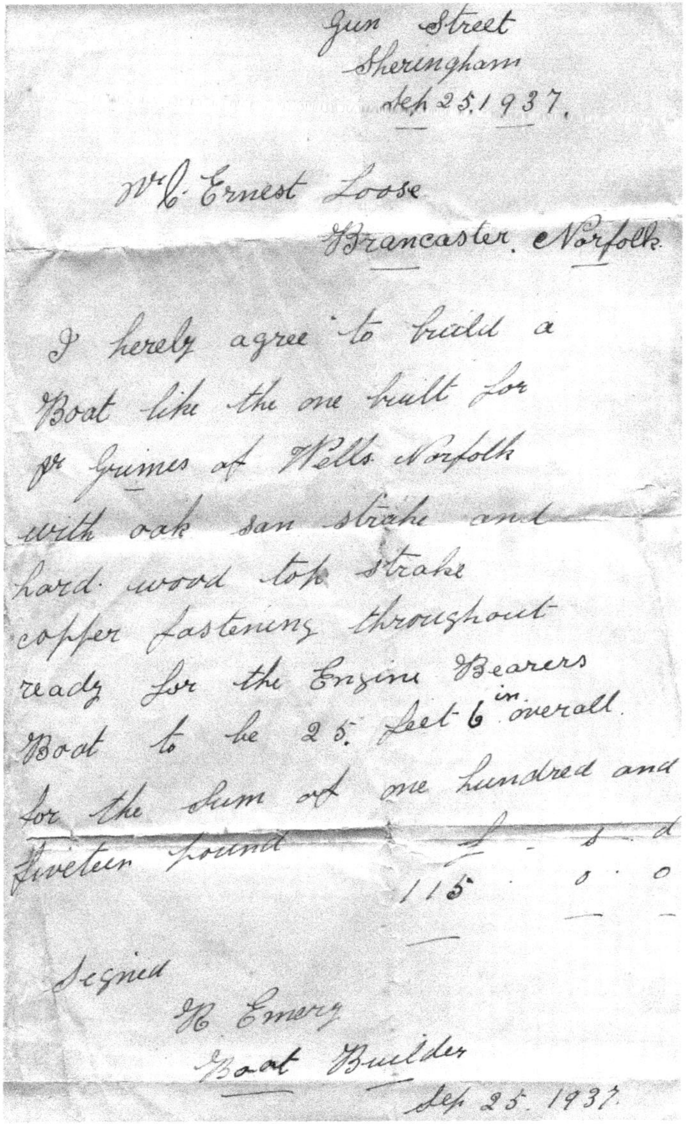

Gun Street
Sheringham
Sep 25. 1937.

Mr C. Ernest Loose

Brancaster. Norfolk.

I hereby agree to build a

Boat like the one built for

Mr Grimes of Wells Norfolk

with oak san strake and

hard wood top strake

copper fastening throughout

ready for the Engine Bearers

Boat to be 25. feet 6 in overall.

for the sum of one hundred and

fifteen pound   £   s   d
                    115   0   0

Signed

H Emery

Boat Builder

Sep 25. 1937.

Two contracts written by Reginald Emery for a 16 foot double-ended crab boat, in 1909 and the whelker *Isabel* in 1937.

Form M.S.2.   LICENCE No. 8448

The Restriction of Construction of Ships Order, 1940, dated January 31st, 1940, made under Regulation 55 of the Defence (General) Regulations, 1939.

LICENCE TO BUILD A SHIP

In pursuance of Article 1 of the Restriction of Construction of Ships Order 1940, the Admiralty hereby authorise (subject to compliance with the conditions mentioned below) the construction by _R. Emery Esq_

_____ (hereinafter called the Builder)

to the order of _Mr. C. Grimes_

of the ship (known as Yard No. _____) of which particulars are given overleaf.

CONDITIONS.

1. The hull and machinery of the ship shall, unless the Admiralty at any time direct otherwise, be constructed in strict accordance with the particulars stated hereon.

2. Hull and machinery specifications shall be forwarded to the Secretary of the Admiralty, (P. Branch II) as soon as practicable, together with a general arrangement plan, all in duplicate.

3. The Builder shall carry out and conform to any alterations in the specifications and plans which the Admiralty may whether on the grant of this licence or at any other time direct in writing to be carried out.

4. The keel of the ship shall be laid by the _31st_ day of _October_ 19_47_ or by such later date as may be endorsed hereon or directed in writing by the Admiralty and construction shall proceed with all despatch with a view to delivery of the ship on about _30th June_ 19_48_, or such late date as may be endorsed or directed as aforesaid.

5. This licence is not transferable and may be revoked by the Admiralty at any time.

6. Immediately on any failure to comply with any of the above conditions this licence shall automatically determine.

NOTE.—The execution after the revocation or determination of the licence of any work for or in respect of the ship will be an offence against Regulation 55 of the Defence (General) Regulations, 1939.

Signed by authority of the Admiralty this _25th_ day of _July_ 19_47_

Admiralty,
    London, S.W.1.

NOTE.—This licence must be returned to the Secretary of the Admiralty (P. Branch II) for cancellation if the licence is determined by reason of the failure to comply with any of the conditions of the licence or is revoked.

M.S. 480—45.

I. Particulars of Vessel.   Type of Ship _Motor Fishing Boat_

Berth on which to be built ___

Dimensions: Length between perpendiculars _30'_

Breadth (moulded) _10'6_   Depth (moulded) _4'6_

Erections ___   Number of decks _

Tonnage (Estimated) Gross Registered ___

Deadweight ___ on ___ Load Draught.

Propelling Machinery: Type _Motor_   Number of Screws ___

Service Horse Power _40 HP_   Estimated Speed on Service ___

Make Size of Engines _Morris_

Size of Boilers ___   Type of Fuel _

Refrigerating Space (if any)—Capacity in cubic feet ___

No. of passengers ___

Safety and Life-Saving Measures: (British Vessels). In accordance with Ministry of Transport Regulations in force at date of completion, or (for Foreign Vessels) as appropriate.

The use of the following timber is authorised by this Licence:—

4 squares 1 x 7 flooring   48 cubic ft. Eng. Larch
8 - 12' x 2½ x 9 Deals   55   "   Oak
_   6   "   Elm_

No guarantee is given or implied that the timber will be available when required.

II. Endorsements of extended period for laying keel.

The period within which keel must be laid is hereby extended

to the ___ day of ___ 19___

III. Endorsements of extended period for delivery.

The period within which delivery must be effected is hereby extended

to the ___ day of ___ 19___

Licence HUL 230 + 231 4 sqa 1 x 7 flooring
_8/12 ft 2½ x 9_
48 ft Larch
55 ft Oak
6 ft Elm.

J. M. Drinkwater
Ron. Oct 6, 1947.

Licence to Build a Ship document, required because of shortages of wood and materials during and following the Second World War. This was for *William Edward*, built in 1949.

Acknowledgements

We are grateful to the retired editor of the *North Norfolk News*, Richard Batson, for casting his eye, and pen, over the text for this book to help our writings flow and become more readable and interesting.

Also special thanks to Peter Stibbons for agreeing, although practically retired, to design our work to the standard that he has gleaned from many years of experience publishing books for dozens of local authors and on many subjects.

Thank you too to Gareth Davies of Poppyland Publishing for all his help and for being willing to get this book printed for you our readers to enjoy.

Research for this story began over forty years ago and over the course of those years many people have contributed memories and loaned precious photographs. Sadly a great number of those generous contributors are no longer with us, but we thank them and remember them always. One substantial contributor and encourager was the late Stanley Craske, Sheringham's true 'Shannock' historian whose tremendous wealth of knowledge and collection of memorabilia and photographs was of great importance to us in the early days.

Reitered North Norfolk newsman and editor, Richard Batson.

Another most supportive and generous of those giving of their knowledge and memories is David Hewitt, boat builder and lover of Norfolk built boats and their history. Much of what is written in these pages has been gleaned from David's encyclopaedic knowledge of local craft and their whereabouts whether a good outcome or sadly not.

Our thanks to James Lyon Fenner for permission to quote from his unpublished 2014 thesis 'British Small Craft: the cultural geographies of mid-twentieth century technology and display'. And thanks also to Robin and Linda West for permission to quote from their 'Henry West Blog', and use of photographs from the Henry West Archive.

Most important of all is our thanks to our families for their support and encouragement over the years that this book has been in preparation.

Authors Malcolm, Michael and Jonathan with the lifeboat *Henry Ramey Upcher*.

Index

Glossary

Adze—a versatile cutting tool, similar to an axe but with the cutting blade perpendicular to the handle rather than horizontal. In use since the earliest of times.

Beach yawl—a sleek, clinker built vessel often used in rescue work on the eastern East Anglian coast

Canvas—a coarse and heavy cloth but can also mean the covering used on vessels or the sails themselves

Clinker, clench—clinker-built, clench-built, when the planks of a vessel overlap each other

Coxswain—for lifeboats, used to describe the commander of the vessel.

Cuddy—a small cabin at the front of the boat.

Deadwood—lower part of the stem or stern posts to which the planking is attached.

Gunwale—the top strake of the planking of a boat.

Hoveller, Hubbler—a larger beach boat used for rescue and salavage work as well as fishing.

Keel—the timber stretching from stem to stern at the base of the boat.

Orruck, ollock—a hole in the top plank of the boat through which an oar could be put.

Quant—a pole for assisting with the launch of boats in rough weather.

Ribs or Timbers—the lateral members from the keel to the top planks, the gunwale of the boat.

Shores—props to hold planks into place until ribs are fitted.

Skeet—wooden device with rollers, taking the keel of boats and enabling them to be moved up and down the beach.

Stem—the front end of a boat.

Stern post—the timber at the back end of a boat.

Stocks—where the keel is laid upon to begin construction of a boat.

Strakes—the horizontal planks of a boat from stem to stern.

Wherry—in an East Anglian context, a type of vessel to navigate the waters of the Broads and its rivers, taking over from the keel-boat in the 18th-19th century.

Wrong—wooden frame placed at intervals throughout the boat to add strength and support engine beds, and to give extra strength for beaching.